HELPING PEOPLE
IN AN AGE OF CONFLICT

TOWARD A NEW PROFESSIONALISM
IN U.S. VOLUNTARY HUMANITARIAN ASSISTANCE

by
Larry Minear

○Inter**Action**®
American Council for Voluntary International Action

To David L. Guyer

*In recognition of his lifelong commitment to
international development and in appreciation
of his leadership in the community of
American private voluntary agencies*

Design by Norie Quintos, typesetting by Barry Weise using Pagemaker
software on Macintosh II equipment.

Printed by Wickersham Printing Company, Lancaster, Pennsylvania

Library of Congress Cataloging in Publication Data

Minear, Larry, 1936-
   Helping People in an Age of Conflict

   Bibliography: p. 96 - 101.
   1. InterAction (Organization: U.S.)
2. Voluntarism -- United States. 3. International relief -- Political aspects. 4. War
relief -- political aspects. I. Title
HV590 . I573 M56 1988   361.7   88-3307
ISBN 0-932140-13-0 (pbk.)

American Council for Voluntary International Action

200 Park Avenue South, New York, NY 10003
1815 H Street, NW, Washington, DC 20006

TABLE OF CONTENTS

FOREWORD

The international community has responded magnificently to major human emergencies, most recently the sub-Saharan African famine of the mid-Eighties. However, the need for humanitarian assistance world-wide is reaching unprecedented levels.

There are fifteen million refugees today and millions of other people who are displaced within their own countries. While droughts and floods, earthquakes and typhoons continue to generate emergency human need, civil strife and other reprehensible actions of human beings and governments are causing more and more human suffering.

Providing assistance to people affected by conflict is not a new challenge, however alarming the increased incidence of current need. What is new is the complexity of the conflicts, the proliferation of actors, and the targeting of humanitarian aid personnel and programs.

Today's conflicts are frequently not the classical confrontations between nations addressed by the Geneva Conventions and traditional international law. They often involve clashes within nations for which ground rules are less clearly established in international practice. In countries such as Ethiopia and the Sudan, El Salvador and Nicaragua, Afghanistan and Sri Lanka, the conflicts themselves make providing aid difficult enough. When aid programs and aid providers themselves become the object of attack, physical or otherwise, the task of meeting human need effectively becomes far more complicated.

Humanitarian assistance, a response to the victims of natural disaster and human conflict, has itself become an object of contention today. The established concept of humanitarian aid is being challenged as such aid becomes more closely linked to geo-political strategies. Military establishments now engage in "humanitarian" activities and many more private politically motivated groups are also getting into the act. The public credibility of aid programs has eroded.

The need for more humanitarian aid worldwide and yet the increased difficulty of providing it effectively are of growing concern to American private and voluntary organizations (PVOs). PVOs are sensing that to accomplish their traditional objectives, they need to match their well-known warm-hearted compassion with hardheaded professional and

4

political expertise. Active more and more in situations where governments are major players and impartiality is difficult to maintain, PVOs are seeking to become more politically astute without sacrificing their apolitical character and mandate, i.e., to provide aid impartially to all in need.

As one way to increase their professionalism and competency, InterAction, a professional association of 112 U.S. PVOs, served as a forum for discussions during the years 1985-87 about the principles and practice of providing humanitarian assistance in conflict situations. This publication reviews those conversations. Rather than setting out InterAction policy, it describes a process of dialogue. It recaps the discussions, summarizes areas of consensus and disagreement, suggests questions which PVO practitioners may wish to take into account, and identifies resources for further study. Its publication is intended to encourage continuing attention to these issues in the coming years.

An InterAction Working Group, chaired by Larry Minear of Church World Service/Lutheran World Relief, planned the dialogue under the guidance of the Public Policy Committee, chaired by John Sewell, President of the Overseas Development Council. Several staff of InterAction and other agencies offered special assistance, including Cindy Cohn, Nancy Iris, Angella VenJohn, Doug Weil, and, in particular, Patty Larson.

Larry Minear wrote this book during a sabbatical leave provided by his agencies. Without his dedication and enthusiasm, it would not have seen the light of day. Publication costs have been underwritten in part by the Christian Children's Fund, Church World Service, the Hunger Project, Lutheran World Relief, the Mennonite Central Committee, the Save the Children Federation, and World Vision, among others.

Readers will surely concur in my view that a better understanding of humanitarian assistance and of the difficulties it faces today is terribly important. It is vital to the welfare of those who need such aid, to the agencies which seek to provide it, and to the public on whose continuing support international humanitarian cooperation depends.

Peter J. Davies, *President and Chief Executive Officer*
American Council for Voluntary International Action (InterAction)
January 25, 1988

CHAPTER I
THE SETTING

"What you and I have been associated with can be called a decade of humanitarian assistance," James N. Purcell, Jr., Director of the State Department's Bureau for Refugee Programs remarked at the 1986 Inter-Action Forum. "The achievements of this decade . . . could not have been accomplished without the indispensable help of the voluntary agencies. Overseas you have shown, time and again, that when the going gets tough, the voluntary agencies get going."

Voluntary agencies have also played a major role, Purcell noted, in resettling over a million refugees in the United States, more than 200,000 in the year 1980 alone. "Taking advantage of your domestic structures — your churches, synagogues, community centers — you expanded your programs to rise to the challenge of this modern exodus. It was a heroic accomplishment."[1]

These were gratifying words from a senior government official in daily touch with the activities of myriad American private and voluntary organizations (PVOs). The words echoed a growing chorus of accolades from international aid workers. The indispensable role of PVOs in cooperative international human needs endeavors is now widely acknowledged. They are in great demand as partners in humanitarian assistance programs, at home and abroad alike.

While welcoming this growing recognition, PVOs are also becoming more self-critical. Their heightened visibility as aid providers has also meant increased scrutiny by governments and the concerned public. "We like to say we're grass-roots oriented, private and non-governmental in nature — in short, that we're good," observed Dr. James Mac-Cracken, Executive Director of the Christian Children's Fund, at the December 1985 InterAction Symposium on "Providing Humanitarian Assistance in Conflict Situations." In their many decades of service, he pointed out, PVOs have aided millions of people in need.

"But people are asking us: Do PVOs know what they are doing? Do they talk to each other? Do they reach the poorest of the poor? Do they allow themselves cynically to be used by governments? Are they really humanitarian? To whom are they accountable? How much of the precious money that is raised is spent on promoting themselves? On what basis do they make appeals?"[2] Such basic questions are commanding increased attention among PVOs, however laudatory the comments from colleagues about their work.

This booklet describes a two-year process of inquiry and reflection by U.S. PVOs through their professional association InterAction. Concerned about what they view as threats to the integrity of such aid, PVOs reviewed the basic principles of humanitarian assistance and the difficulties it faces today. Events abroad and in the United States gave the dialogue special urgency and concreteness.

Conflict Ascendent Worldwide

On January 10, 1985 at its headquarters in Geneva, Switzerland, Alexandre Hay, President of the International Committee of the Red Cross (ICRC), launched "An Appeal for Humanity." During the Eighties the ICRC had observed an escalating level of violence world-wide. The number of conflicts, their duration, and the toll in human suffering were on the rise. Many conflicts showed little hope of peaceful or prompt resolution. Functioning exclusively in conflict situations, the ICRC is a respected bellwether on such matters.

"Little, if any, effect," Hay said, had come of a more modest ICRC appeal earlier in the decade that "in all times and all circumstances the universally recognized rules of international law and humanitarian principles should be safeguarded."[3] He noted that appeals to the parties in particular conflicts — in Iran and Iraq, Afghanistan, the Western Sahara, Kampuchea, and (regarding its occupied territories) Israel — had produced distressingly few positive results.

The 1985 ICRC Appeal for Humanity, therefore, looked beyond individual humanitarian emergencies and their assaults on human dignity to seek rekindled respect among governments and peoples for international law and reinvigorated programs providing succor to the victims of violence. "Only a general mobilization may prevent these tragic forecasts [of escalating violence] from becoming realities," Hay observed. "Everyone must be conscious of the urgent, dramatic need for a vast uprising of humanity and solidarity that is essential in the face of actual and potential folly of human violence."[4]

The ICRC, which has played a key role for more than a century in the development, promotion, and observance of international humanitarian law, was committing itself to redoubled efforts. Priority would be placed on promoting the ratification and observance by governments of the Geneva Convention and Protocols, on educating political leaders and military officials to their humanitarian obligations, and on encouraging the international public to insist on more effective humanitarian action. The ICRC would also continue to augment the size and professionalism of its own staff to meet its burgeoning responsibilities in the resolution of conflict and the protection of the imprisoned.

The disturbing trends noted by the ICRC were confirmed by the Independent Commission on International Humanitarian Issues, an international group of experts which during the Eighties has undertaken research and education on various forces which threaten the human condition, including famine, environmental degradation, human displacement, and migration. The Commission established a Working Group whose report and papers were published in *Modern Wars: The Humanitarian Challenge.* Excerpts from the Commission's work are contained in the feature boxes on pages 9 and 41.

"The history of humanity is one long succession of wars and conflicts," says the Commission's report, "Humanitarian Law at a Time of Failing National and International Consensus." Major past wars such as World Wars I and II have given way to a host of local wars and internal conflicts, in part due to "the weakness and precariousness of newly independent States faced with the problems of underdevelopment and a host of political contradictions and socio-economic difficulties."[5]

"For a decade or two," the report continued, "conflicts have clearly been more frequent, more serious, and more radicalized. The Iran-Iraq war has been going on longer than World War II. Prisoners of war in conflicts like the Ogaden or Western Sahara have been held for over twice the period of detention of World War II prisoners. The fate of refugees in the camps on the Thai-Kampuchean border reminds us more and more of the situation in Palestinian camps, dragging on and on for years with no solution in sight. .... Situations are becoming more complex, ideologies more extreme and crises have a greater tendency to culminate in war."[6]

Modern wars, too, the Commission reported, have taken an increasing toll on civilians. While only five percent of the casualties in World War I were civilian, seventy-five percent of World War II casualties were such, and in some contemporary wars, over ninety percent of the casualties are civilians.[7] In fact, traditional distinctions between civilians and combatants have become blurred. Civilians have themselves been targeted in recent conflicts. International law is therefore seeking to fashion ground rules for the now more endemic "internal disturbances and tensions" not clearly addressed by existing international convention.[8]

A Time of Violence

We live in a time of violence, of erosion of family structure, of centrifugal forces at the national level, of acute conflict in labour relations. Our traditional beliefs are shadowed by doubts. General anxiety has become the lot of man in the face of scientific, technological and even medical progress. Ethical barriers have broken down, fundamental moral values are questioned and man is engulfed by waves of fear and insecurity. In our own conscience, in the family, at school, at work, in the community, in the country, and finally in international relations, negative forces are at work. The national consensus is being eroded and the international consensus seriously undermined.

The erosion is visible at every level. The proliferation of authoritarian regimes or the quest for charismatic leaders are a reflection of our fear and uncertainty. Fear pervades human society. This is why people look for 'the strong man whom providence would send to dissipate human anxieties.' The contemporary world seems fascinated by the totalitarian model which deifies those in power. Governments rule and citizens obey: such is the individual and collective reflex today.

Independent Commission on International Humanitarian Issues, Humanitarian Law at a Time of Failing National and International Consensus.

The untoward international environment of the Eighties, particularly the emerging politicization of humanitarian aid activities, was also becoming a concern to international non-governmental organizations (NGOs). Many are members of the International Council of Voluntary Agencies (ICVA), a Geneva-based association of 85 international, regional, and national NGOs and groupings of NGOs. A number of U.S. PVOs and InterAction itself are also members.

Early in 1983, the ICVA secretariat prepared a discussion paper for the ICVA governing board entitled "Humanitarian Organizations and Politics." It examined various definitions of the terms *humanitarian* and *political*, reviewed the political implications of humanitarian activities, and explored some of the tensions between non-political aid activities and NGO advocacy with governments. A number of ICVA agencies have continued their interest in the issues and ICVA itself is returning to the subject by co-hosting with the international Red Cross movement a conference in 1988, described on page 50.

Humanitarian Assistance to the Contras

If the crisis in international humanitarian action provided the general backdrop for the InterAction dialogue, the specific question of humanitarian assistance for the Nicaraguan Contras sparked direct PVO engagement with the issues. In early 1985 the Reagan Administration requested, and in the summer Congress approved, $27 million in "humanitarian assistance" to the Nicaraguan armed opposition. The request sought "food, clothing, medicine, and other humanitarian assistance" for Contra soldiers and dependents. Lethal materiel was excluded; "non-lethal" items such as tents, communications equipment, and vehicles were not.

The issue of Contra aid divided the PVO community. Some PVOs felt Contra aid deserved their active support. Others held that as part of a flawed U.S. policy toward Central America, it should be opposed. Some believed that while it was beyond their competence to address broader questions of U.S. policy toward the region, PVOs should actively contest the notion that aid of any sort to combatants could qualify as humanitarian. Still others resisted being drawn into the fray, although remaining uneasy with the loose use of the term with which they as humanitarian agencies were identified.

Preliminary discussions among PVOs within the InterAction Public Policy Committee in the spring of 1985 produced general consensus at several points. It would be helpful to review "first principles" of humanitarian assistance. Any pronouncements, however, should be universal and generic rather than country-specific. Given the sensitivity of the issues, individual agencies or groups of agencies addressing Contra aid should do so on their own, not on behalf of InterAction.

The emphasis in the InterAction discussions was indeed on first principles. The draft Statement on Humanitarian Assistance which circulated among PVOs (Appendix I) did not mention Contra aid. However, InterAction did not adopt policy on humanitarian assistance since even the generic Statement did not achieve the necessary unanimity among member agencies.

Divergent viewpoints on humanitarian aid to the Contras notwithstanding, the InterAction process proved a constructive one. It stimulated individual agencies to review and modify their policies. Several PVOs communicated their views individually to policy-makers. One informal PVO grouping voiced its opinion that Contra aid was neither humanitarian nor appropriate.[9] Thus while PVO alarm over the politicization of aid in Central America helped provide a place on the crowded InterAction agenda for the issue of humanitarian assistance, the process did not, as some PVOs had feared and other PVOs had hoped, line up the PVO community in opposition to Contra aid.

PVO Involvement in Humanitarian Aid

In order to structure a dialogue on humanitarian assistance issues suited to the needs of InterAction members, the Public Policy Committee mailed a questionnaire in the fall of 1985 to InterAction's hundred-plus members. The data generated, reprinted in Appendix II, became the basis for the InterAction activities described in Chapter II and analyzed in Chapter III.

Sixteen of the twenty PVOs responding indicated that they provided humanitarian assistance. However, the survey found widely divergent understandings of such aid. For some PVOs, humanitarian aid consisted specifically of emergency relief assistance; for others, it included the ingredients of self-reliant development. Three of the four agencies which said they did not provide humanitarian aid were nevertheless involved in development or other human needs activities which many of those answering in the affirmative considered humanitarian. In fact, the single need which most agencies articulated was for a clearer definition of humanitarian assistance. "Does the PVO community," one respondent asked, "accept the definition . . . provided in the Geneva Conventions?"

Of the sixteen agencies which provided humanitarian assistance, twelve had working definitions of such aid. Fifteen indicated that questions about the nature of such aid had figured in recent programming decisions. Seventeen reported that questions related to the nature of humanitarian assistance had been the subject of staff discussions. Fourteen sensed growing public concern about the politicization of humanitarian aid and only nine felt they had adequate resources to answer such questions as they arose.

The survey also suggested the considerable extent to which U.S. PVOs cooperate with other humanitarian aid providers. All twenty respondents had worked with PVOs indigenous to developing countries, seventeen with the U.S. Agency for International Development (AID), fifteen with the governments of developing countries, ten with the State Department and the United Nations High Commissioner for Refugees (UNHCR), and five with the U.N. Disaster Relief Organization (UNDRO) and the International Committee for the Red Cross (ICRC).

PVOs had also collaborated with other U.N. agencies (mentioned were the World Food Council, the Food and Agriculture Organization, the U.N. Development Program, and the International Fund for Agricultural Development), the U.S. Information Agency, governments of other aid-providing nations, local communities, and other U.S. PVOs. American PVOs clearly provide humanitarian aid in collaboration with many other groups, though the degree of actual coordination was not apparent from the survey.

The completion of questionnaires by only twenty InterAction agencies limited the representativeness of the data. However, the results provided an impression of PVO involvement and interests in humanitarian activities. The questionnaire also elicited suggestions of specific regions and countries about which discussion would be helpful and identified staff people to help plan future activities. Several agencies which did not complete the questionnaire still became actively involved in the InterAction dialogue and some without overseas activities also participated. As the dialogue proceeded, the substantial interest generated bore out the impression given by the survey that the issue of providing humanitarian assistance in conflict situations was indeed a significant concern for the InterAction family of PVOs.

Prevailing Public Opinion

The publication in early 1987 of a survey of American views on international development confirmed the importance of humanitarian assistance to the American people but reflected disturbing public perceptions about the effectiveness of such aid. Co-sponsored by InterAction and the Overseas Development Council, the mid-1986 poll involved telephone surveys of 2,400 randomly selected adult Americans and five hundred "activists," interviews with thirteen Members of Congress and their aides, and four group discussions in three U.S. cities.

While the views of the general public and the activists differed on some points, the survey found that a majority of Americans favor helping people in developing countries. For most, "humanitarian concern appears to be the major basis for interest" in doing so.[10] Most respondents favored helping through economic rather than military aid; among varieties of economic assistance, humanitarian aid enjoyed particular support. "Relief for victims of disasters such as floods, droughts, and earthquakes was given high priority by the largest percentage (74%) of the general public. However, longer-term development programs perceived to deliver assistance most directly to needy people — programs such as health care, education on family planning and providing birth control, helping farmers, and U.S. volunteer programs — were also rated as high priority by a majority of the respondents."[11]

The survey reported that "The major reasons given by Americans for favoring economic assistance reflect a humanitarian desire to help other people. Economic and political reasons ... are generally far less important." For fifty-three percent of the general public, support for economic assistance was related to humanitarian concerns or feelings of responsibility. Some twenty-eight percent expressed "[p]olitical and strategic rationales for supporting U.S. economic assistance — such as making and keeping allies, discouraging communism, fostering democracy, and promoting world peace." Fourteen percent of the public supported economic assistance for economic reasons such as promoting growth in developing countries and the United States.[12]

The survey also detected widespread skepticism about whether U.S. aid reaches those who need it and "a growing degree of pessimism about progress made in improving the lives of the poor in developing countries."[13] Eighty-one percent of the public endorsed the statement that "Governments in Third World countries are largely to blame for creating their own problems through poor planning."[14] Eighty-eight percent agreed that "aid is frequently misused by foreign governments," eighty-five percent that "A large part of aid is wasted by the U.S. bureaucracy."[15] Fifty-three percent of the public agreed that "The problems in developing countries are so overwhelming that anything the United States does is just a drop in the bucket."[16] Most felt that living conditions there had stagnated or deteriorated during the past ten years.

The lack of public confidence in aid programs was particularly noteworthy. People were asked whether they had "a great deal, just some, or little confidence that most of the money people give to private organizations (like CARE and Save the Children) reaches needy people in other countries." An identical question followed about "the money for assistance that the United States government sends overseas." Seventeen percent of the respondents expressed *a great deal of confidence* in private aid programs, while seven percent indicated the same level of confidence in U.S. government programs. Forty-two percent expressed *just some confidence* in private aid programs, forty-five percent in government programs. Thirty-six percent had *little confidence* in private programs, forty-six percent in government programs. Five percent didn't know or didn't answer the question about private aid programs, four percent about government programs. Only roughly half of the public thus expressed confidence that PVO and U.S. government aid programs are effective.[17]

Drought, Fighting, and Famine

In this age of the green revolution, with crop yields skyrocketing, drought no longer automatically means famine. India, for example, is now in the midst of its worst drought in decades, but because it has a food surplus and a relatively organized system for feeding the hungry, few are expected to starve. Usually it is the combination of drought, mismanagement and civil war that brings famine. Ethiopia is afflicted with all three.

Getting the food to the hungry is made more difficult by inadequate port facilities, poor or nonexistent roads and insufficient planes and trucks to transport food to rural areas. But the biggest block in the pipeline is civil strife. The two strongest insurgent armies are in Tigre and Eritrea, the provinces hit hardest by the drought. Eritrea has been in rebellion against the government ever since it was annexed by Ethiopia in 1962, and a guerrilla movement began building in Tigre in 1977.

Time Cover Story on Famine in Ethiopia, 21 December 1987.

Also disturbing from a PVO standpoint was an apparently waning preference for private over governmental efforts, though people generally expressed greater confidence in private than in government aid. A somewhat similar question fifteen years earlier had found that fifty-seven percent of the public favored assistance through PVOs, the Peace Corps, the Red Cross, and UNICEF while only twenty-two percent wished to see U.S. foreign aid go "directly to the governments of the countries themselves."[18] The more recent survey found in its group discussions that "While Americans do not see much difference between governmental and private programs, they do perceive differences between the reasons why the U.S. government and private agencies get involved in the Third World." PVO activities were generally viewed as having primarily humanitarian purposes, U.S. government aid as tending to be "motivated by, and allocated according to, political, strategic, or economic objectives."[19]

In sum, there is widespread humanitarian concern among the American people. Fully eighty-nine percent of the general public agreed with the statement that "Wherever people are hungry or poor, we ought to do what we can to help them."[19] The public also supported aid appropriate to those needs and given for humanitarian rather than economic or political/strategic reasons. However, skepticism about the utility of such aid also appears widespread, with relatively little discrimination among different kinds of aid agencies. The negative attitudes expressed toward governments represent a major challenge to PVOs in generating public understanding of the more frequent dealings with governments needed, the InterAction dialogue suggests, by PVOs who wish to provide effective humanitarian aid today.

Confirming Events

Interlaced throughout the two-year humanitarian assistance dialogue were events which confirmed the importance of the discussions taking place. Indeed, the InterAction dialogue probably attracted widespread PVO participation because it coincided with, and provided an opportunity to reflect upon, difficulties being experienced by agencies in their aid programs. Recurring media treatment of humanitarian emergencies stimulated increased public interest in the issues as well.

As the InterAction exercise got underway in 1985, the center of international humanitarian concern was **sub-Saharan Africa**, where some 150 million persons were estimated to be at serious nutritional risk, seven million in Ethiopia alone. A massive international famine relief effort was mounted by governments, United Nations agencies, and private organizations. Sustained media coverage of particularly hard-hit countries and mass fund-raising activities by groups such as USA for Africa and Live Aid/Band Aid brought the humanitarian emergency home to many in the U.S. and abroad. The multifaceted involvement of U.S. PVOs has been chronicled in an earlier InterAction monograph.[21]

As improved harvests returned in 1986-87 to many parts of the region and attention shifted to reconstruction and famine prevention, the humanitarian crisis continued in Ethiopia, the Sudan, Mozambique, and Angola. Civil strife in each of these countries underscored the linkage between hunger and conflict. Political and military interference with aid efforts was widely reported and lamented. Whether the U.S. should provide humanitarian assistance to the Marxist government of Mozambique, like earlier discussions about the provision of such aid to the Marxist government of Ethiopia, was the subject of public debate. Linkages between "natural" disasters such as food shortages and the policies and priorities of governments in agriculture, environment, human settlements, and human rights became better understood.

The tragic situation of blacks in South Africa also received extensive coverage. As pressure from within South Africa to dismantle apartheid increased, more public attention was directed to appropriate ways of encouraging that process from outside. Issues such as whether the U.S. should impose economic sanctions against South Africa and whether, and how, U.S. government aid should be provided to black South Africans came in for considerable attention. The involvement in the struggle of countless children, imprisoned in large numbers for opposing racial segregation, dramatized the humanitarian emergency.

Attention to conflicts in **Central America** and their human casualties may have upstaged the situation in sub-Saharan Africa during the years 1985-87. Civil strife had created widespread human suffering in El Salvador, Guatemala, and Nicaragua and growing refugee populations in neighboring countries. The well-being of ethnic minorities as well as those in contested areas was imperiled. Not only did civilian casualties mount into the tens of thousands; a substantial number of international and indigenous humanitarian aid personnel experienced harassment, injury, and death. Aid agencies seeking to respond to the casualties and causes of the conflict found themselves caught up in it. The presence of many U.S. citizens in the region as aid personnel and as visitors on fact-finding and solidarity missions lent immediacy to Central American issues. Conversely, the presence of many Central American refugees in the United States and efforts to provide them with services and sanctuary received considerable public attention.

U.S. policy toward Central America was also a matter of daily media attention. The imposition in 1984 of a U.S. embargo on trade with

Nicaragua, exempting humanitarian items, had sparked public debate. The provision in 1985 of $27 million in "humanitarian assistance" to the Contras was followed by additional requests for, and heated discussions of, such aid. The growing reference to such aid as "non-lethal" mirrored the concern expressed by some PVOs for more precision in nomenclature. The State Department gave serious consideration in mid-1986 to declaring the United Nicaraguan Opposition, the Contra political and military arm, a PVO so that it could receive Food for Peace and other U.S. government aid.[22] The 1987 Iran-Contra hearings reviewed the effort by Administration officials to encourage private donations to the Contras. In a related development, two Americans who had solicited such contributions "pleaded guilty to criminal charges that they conspired to defraud the U.S. government by using tax deductible contributions for contra military activities."[23]

The judgment of the International Court of Justice in June, 1986 in the case brought by Nicaragua against the United States spoke to both the positive attributes of humanitarian aid and the violation of international law by U.S. actions. (The feature box on page 22 contains excerpts from the Court's ruling.) Reviewing the broad spectrum definition of humanitarian assistance in the U.S. Contra aid legislation, the World Court concluded that if such aid were to be authentically humanitarian, "not only must it be limited to the purposes hallowed in the practice of the Red Cross, namely 'to prevent and alleviate human suffering', and 'to protect life and health and to ensure respect for the human being'; it must also, and above all, be given without discrimination to all in need in Nicaragua, not merely to the contras and their dependents."[24] The Reagan Administration rejected the Court's judgment and jurisdiction.

Humanitarian emergencies in **Asia** also claimed ongoing public attention during the mid-Eighties. The needs of Afghans in Pakistan — the world's largest refugee population, numbering an estimated 3.3 million at the end of 1986 — became a prominent international and American preoccupation. The continued presence at the year's end of more than 250,000 Kampucheans in refugee camps along the Thai border and the problems of access to them by aid agency personnel were also significant concerns. The needs of persons within Kampuchea and Vietnam, whose governments were ostracized by much of the international community, remained major, though they received less attention. Ethnic tension in Sri Lanka was also in the news.

In the **Middle East**, the continuing strife in Lebanon, which by 1987 had claimed more than an estimated 430,000 civilian casualties, substantial coverage. The condition of refugees in camps, which had been the subject of attacks and sieges, underscored the problems of access by relief personnel to people in need. The plight of seventeen persons (eight of them Americans) remaining hostage in Lebanon as of the end of November 1987, and the pleas that they be released on humanitarian grounds, were recurrent themes of news coverage during this period. The Iran-Iraq war, which had resulted in mind-boggling numbers of casualties, many of them civilian, received mounting coverage during these years, as did stepped up U.N. efforts in 1987 to mediate a cease-fire.

The InterAction dialogue thus took place at a time of mounting conflict world-wide and of ambivalent American perceptions of the effectiveness of humanitarian assistance efforts. Highly publicized situations of need around the globe, in which PVOs were both increasingly recognized as major actors and yet more and more constrained in their actions, lent urgency to their review of the principles of humanitarian assistance and the ground rules for providing it more effectively.

The dialogue itself involved a number of separate events, each building on the needs of member PVOs expressed in the InterAction questionnaire. The first was a Symposium on "Providing Humanitarian Assistance in Conflict Situations," held in Washington, D.C. in December 1985. This was followed by an extended discussion of the issues at the May 1986 InterAction Annual Forum in McAfee, New Jersey. The Forum led in turn to discussions with senior State Department officials in December 1986. Events in 1987 involved discussions with the Defense Department and the concerned public. A description of the dialogue is the subject of Chapter II. An analysis of the issues is provided in Chapter III.

A World of Suffering Beyond Description

Today [articulating] the prophetic voice, more often than not, makes us uncomfortable. . . . But World Vision, I say, cannot be silent. Our work takes us into a world of war, famine, poverty, disease and injustice beyond description. We work in a world of refugees in unprecedented number, of children dying at a rate of 40,000 a day, of hope deferred, indeed, hope forgotten. We must speak for those who have no voice, for the 15 million children a year who die in physical and spiritual darkness.

Robert A. Seiple, President, World Vision United States, 1987.

CHAPTER II
THE DIALOGUE

In the spring of 1985, PVOs associated with InterAction began a series of intensive discussions covering a two-year period about the principles and practice of humanitarian assistance. This chapter recaps the major events in the dialogue. The next chapter analyzes the key issues which emerged.

Activities in 1985

In early 1985, several PVOs approached InterAction's Public Policy Committee with concerns about the politicization of humanitarian assistance. The Reagan Administration had requested congressional approval of what it termed humanitarian assistance for the Nicaraguan Contras. Was such aid humanitarian? Would it alleviate suffering or create additional hardship? Would it affect the work of private humanitarian organizations active in Central America and elsewhere?

To review these issues, InterAction's Public Policy Committee formed a Working Group on Humanitarian Assistance, open to interested member PVOs and accountable to the Committee. Agencies participating included the African-American Institute, the American Friends Service Committee, American Near East Refugee Aid, CARE, Catholic Relief Services, Church World Service, the Presiding Bishop's Fund for World Relief of the Episcopal Church, Lutheran World Relief, the Mennonite Central Committee, the Save the Children Federation, and the U.S. Committee for Refugees/American Council for Nationalities Services.

The Working Group met regularly to review developments and to plan activities. Its work, facilitated by InterAction staff, structured the PVO community's ongoing engagement with humanitarian assistance issues. Chaired by Larry Minear of Church World Service/Lutheran World Relief, it was made up of PVO staff based in Washington. The activities it orchestrated engaged PVO officials and staff from across the country.

The concern about the politicization of humanitarian aid extended beyond InterAction. At its May 1985 meeting, the AID Advisory Committee on Voluntary Foreign Aid, a group of leaders from the private sector charged with facilitating communication between PVOs and AID, reviewed the issue of Contra aid. "We were unanimously and seriously concerned about the possibility of AID involvement in serving as the administrator of this assistance," Committee Chair E. Morgan Williams, President of the National Cooperative Business Association, reported to AID Administrator M. Peter McPherson. The Committee saw such involvement as affecting "AID's credibility in the Third World, with our friendly allies, and, of course, with the American Private Voluntary Agencies."[1]

It was evident that humanitarian assistance issues required the attention of the PVO community beyond those serving on the Public Policy Committee or its Humanitarian Assistance Working Group. At its September meeting, the Public Policy Committee therefore authorized the Working Group to plan a one-day discussion on humanitarian aid before year's end. The result was a Symposium on "Providing Humanitarian Assistance in Conflict Situations: The Challenge for PVOs," held December 2, 1985 at the national headquarters of the American Red Cross in Washington, D.C.

The Symposium had three basic objectives. It sought to review the principles which guide PVO work, to examine the international ground rules applicable to the functioning of PVOs in conflict situations, and to seek consensus on an eventual InterAction policy statement on humanitarian assistance. To encourage reflection on the issues among InterAction members, the meeting was closed to other PVOs, academics, government officials, and the press. On such a complex and sensitive issue, the Working Group believed, the first order of business was for the organized PVO community to do its own homework.

Thus the group that gathered in Washington was, in the words of David Guyer, President of the Save the Children Federation, who chaired the Symposium, "our family around the table." Fifty participants from thirty-four PVOs engaged in an intensive and task-oriented day of discussions. "It is important for the PVO community, both old and new hands," Guyer told the group, "to review periodically the nature and provision of humanitarian assistance." The Symposium was particularly timely, he observed, given the mounting need for humanitarian aid, the growing public and congressional interest in it, and the increasing difficulties of providing it in complex and politicized circumstances.

The session progressed from the historical to the contemporary, from the general to the specific. The day began with reflections on PVO traditions as humanitarian aid providers by James MacCracken, Executive Director of the Christian Children's Fund. He recalled long-term PVO involvement in humanitarian aid: a century and a half of assistance to Jewish refugees, post-World War I help to devastated Europe, aid during the Peking famine of 1927, Bundles for Britain and the United China Relief during World War II, and post-war reconstruction in Europe. In more recent years, he recalled, PVOs had provided the model for what later became the U.S. Public Law 480 food assistance program. PVOs had also aided people in Berlin, Taiwan, Biafra, Bangladesh, Southeast Asia, the Sahel, the Horn of Africa, and elsewhere around the globe.

"We've come a long way," MacCracken observed, from the early days of missionary outreach to the current working partnership with governments and United Nations organizations. Yet as the issues have become more complex, he noted, PVOs have found it harder to function with professionalism. PVOs had successfully aided in the reconstruction of Europe following World War II, resettling millions of displaced persons in a dramatic response to a black-and-white situation. Humanitarian action today, on the other hand, is set in a far more complex and political context. It is more vulnerable, MacCracken said, to the influence of governments and to the dangers of the conflicts themselves — witness the hostage status of Father Lawrence Jenco of Catholic Relief Services in the Middle East.[2] In this new and troubling environment, the PVO community needs to define "the ethics of humanitarianism" in a way which affirms the "basic verities" embodied in PVO traditions yet guides the community toward responsible action in a more complex time.

Against this backdrop, the Symposium's attention turned to the context in which current humanitarian aid activities are set. The international setting was provided by Jean-Jacques Surbeck, New York-based North American delegate of the International Committee of the Red Cross. Joseph A. Mitchell, Washington attorney and former director of AID's Office of Foreign Disaster Assistance, commented on the domestic context.

Surbeck presented the Geneva Conventions and Protocols as providing an internationally recognized framework for the activities of the International Committee of the Red Cross and other private humanitarian assistance providers. While these instruments provide no standard, all-purpose definition of humanitarian aid, they recognize the essential qualities of such aid to be the following:

1. **humanitarian,** that is, "concerned with the condition of man considered solely as a human being, regardless of his value as a military, political, professional or other unit;"

2. **impartial,** that is, "dispensing help, relief and care on the basis of the actual needs of all victims, whoever they are;" and

3. **accountable,** "first and foremost to the victims themselves" but also to the authorities of the territory concerned and to the donors.

Humanitarian assistance was intended exclusively for civilians and for captured, wounded, or otherwise incapacitated military personnel.

The Purpose of Humanitarian Assistance

The characteristics [of humanitarian assistance] were indicated in the first and second of the fundamental principles declared by the Twentieth International Conference of the Red Cross, that

'the Red Cross, born of a desire to bring assistance without discrimination to the wounded on the battlefield, endeavours — in its international and national capacity — to prevent and alleviate human suffering wherever it may be found. Its purpose is to protect life and health and to ensure respect for the human being. It promotes understanding, friendship, co-operation and lasting peace amongst all peoples'

and that 'It makes no discrimination as to nationality, race, religious beliefs, class or political opinions. It endeavours only to relieve suffering, giving priority to the most urgent cases of distress.'

Judgment of the International Court of Justice in the Case of Nicaragua v. the United States of America, 1986.

Surbeck expressed concern that humanitarian aid was in danger of losing its traditionally impartial character. "Until recently," he observed, "there seemed to be a vague consensus as to what was to be understood by 'humanitarian', namely, any activity aimed at helping people in need. ... The strength of genuine humanitarian work until now has rested to a large extent on the fact that, owing to its nature, it is in essence considered a-political . . . and can therefore proceed unimpeded." He noted with concern the recent tendency to use "this adjective for purposes which border dangerously close to obvious political waters. If this trend takes momentum," he stated, "all organizations involved in genuine humanitarian work might find themselves in a difficult, if not risky, position in their field operation."[3]

Mitchell reviewed the legal and political setting in which U.S. PVOs as aid practitioners function. While U.S. law contains no precise definition of humanitarian assistance, he noted, the U.S. is a party to the Geneva Conventions and bound by international law and custom.[4]

U.S. law and regulations, he observed, both encourage the humanitarian work of PVOs and limit their freedom of action. "PVOs greatly assist in the achieving of U.S. foreign policy objectives, and in most cases, the 'humanitarian assistance' objectives of the PVO itself." Yet the effect of U.S. law and regulations, he noted, is that "the PVO gives up ... at least some independence and free initiative in the process. PVOs must conform organizationally, procedurally, and programmatically to many varied administrative and reporting requirements" of the U.S. government.[5]

Mitchell, too, expressed serious concern about an erosion in the traditional understanding of humanitarian assistance. "With the forming of new [U.S.] private organizations during the last year ... to fund and transport 'humanitarian assistance' to the Contra forces in Nicaragua, and [with] the recent U.S. congressional authorization of 'humanitarian aid' to those same forces, serious new questions arise as to common understandings and proper roles of PVOs." Mitchell encouraged "PVOs as individual agencies and as a community ... to assist in providing Congress and the American public a historical and present consensus on this issue."[6]

The Symposium then turned to case studies of PVO principles in action, one historical and one contemporary. The first concerned the provision of aid to Kampucheans during the 1979-84 period, the second of aid to the Contras in 1984-85. Symposium participants had been provided with background readings on each.

The historical setting of the Kampuchean situation, in which some five million persons had required emergency assistance in 1979, was reviewed by Joseph Short, former Executive Director of Oxfam America. (His views are also elaborated in the feature box on page 25.) A current update was provided by Scott Leiper, Deputy Coordinator of the United Nations Border Relief Operation, in which fourteen PVOs were cooperating with the World Food Program and the Thai Government to provide assistance to Kampuchean refugees.

The effort to aid Kampucheans, both within their own country and in border camps within Thailand, raised both ethical and practical questions for PVOs. They included the following:

1. In conflicts, which by definition involve situations in which adversaries face off against each other, how can PVOs themselves avoid taking sides, thereby cutting themselves off from those in need? Agencies assisting on the Thai border were unable to help within Kampuchea; those working within were barred from Thailand. Should there be a strategy to assure that through the sum total of the activities of individual aid providers, the needs of all are met, irrespective of geographical location or political affiliation?

2. In a situation in which various national interests (for example, those of the U.S., Thailand, and Vietnam) are perceived to run counter to the interests of persons requiring humanitarian aid, should PVOs become active champions with governments and the international public of human interests which are being compromised?

3. Can and should PVOs be scrupulously apolitical in some respects and avowedly political in others? For example, should PVOs, which are obligated to provide assistance to all in need, at the same time intervene with governments to allow assistance to reach its destinations? To what extent should PVOs challenge the governments on whose consent their continued relief operations depend? How public should they be in whatever criticism they feel is necessary?

The case study on PVO assistance to the Contras generated even more lively debate. Sharing the panel were three persons with experience in Latin America: Vicki Kemper, News Editor of *Sojourners* Magazine; Tom Hawk, a former Country Director for World Relief in Honduras; and Ed Marasciulo, Executive Vice President of the Pan American Development Foundation.

Humanitarian aid to Nicaraguans in Honduras, in Kemper's view, had become politicized. In order to encourage refugees to become more self-reliant, agencies such as the U.N. High Commissioner for Refugees and the American PVO World Relief, which operated camps at the standard fifty-kilometer distance from the Nicaraguan border, had reduced their levels of refugee assistance. Their approach was undercut, however, by the availability of generous assistance from newer relief groups such as Friends of the Americas, The Nicaraguan Refugee Fund, the Christian Broadcasting Network, and the World Anti-Communist League. The concern of these groups, Kemper said, was not the welfare of the refugees, who would have been safer and more able to meet their own needs farther from the border. Had the beneficiairies not been Contra dependents, Contra sympathizers, and Contras themselves, she said, these relief groups would not have taken an interest.[7]

Politics and Assistance to Kampucheans

Humanitarian aid in disaster situations often has political implications; this seems especially so in the case of Kampuchea where the struggle for governmental control of that country continues, where the near demise of an entire nation derived from political and diplomatic failures, and where even today the ultimate security of the people cries out for political and negotiated settlements.

With considerable justification, it has been argued that food to aid the Kampucheans in Thailand was diverted to bolster the resurgence of the Pol Pot forces — and that humanitarian aid inside Kampuchea indirectly fortified the present Vietnamese occupation. Because humanitarian aid may affect the balance of political forces within and among countries, diplomats of any nationality are tempted to block humanitarian aid to those people in "enemy" areas; but as the case of Kampuchea also demonstrates, they may temper their political cynicism with human kindness, or at least a more "flexible pragmatism." . . .

What might the humanitarian-aid agencies have further done to overcome or sidestep the political obstacles to meeting the life-or-death needs of literally hundreds of thousands of people in Thailand and Kampuchea? Humanitarian-aid agencies operating in disaster situations must hone in on the survival and emergency needs of people without primary reference to ultimate political goals and consequences. This response is more than rhetoric and easier said than done; it is an approach that will not please and may even antagonize the proponents of "playing hardball with the enemy."

The corollary is that in an area of military conflict humanitarian-aid organizations have a moral and practical obligation to assure that the aid goes effectively and efficiently only to noncombatants. If humanitarian-aid organizations either deliberately or unwittingly use their resources to advance particular political or military objectives, they can readily forfeit their moral and practical standing that enables them to play a useful role.

"Voluntary Aid Inside Kampuchea," by Joel R. Charny and Joseph Short.

Hawk's experience bore out Kemper's concerns. Some 17,500 Miskito Indian refugees in Honduras assisted by World Relief had been well on their way to self-reliance. However, with the availability of overly generous U.S. government and private aid along the border, some 4,000 refugees had left ready-to-harvest fields in favor of closer-to-the-border areas.[8] The central issue was not that of competition among relief groups for an opportunity to assist the refugees. It was rather one of basic principle: should refugees be used by relief groups to advance a political agenda? Hawk also described World Relief's efforts to establish its independence from U.S. foreign policy in the area.

Marasciulo, a career AID official in Latin America before becoming a PVO executive, found nothing unusual in the fact that, given the history of U.S. intervention in the region, generous assistance was now being provided by the American people and government. He did raise a concern about the array of new private groups soliciting tax-exempt funds from Central American exiles and others in the U.S. to advance a clearly political agenda. He encouraged InterAction to become more concerned about whether these were legitimate humanitarian assistance organizations and urged more circumspection in PVO dealings with the U.S. and other governments in such circumstances.

The discussion dealt with whether humanitarian assistance, in so complex and politicized a situation, could remain apolitical. One Symposium participant suggested that PVO activities could preserve their humanitarian character only if PVOs left *unaddressed* the reasons humanitarian assistance was needed. PVOs should take a Hippocratic oath, in fact, to keep political considerations from intruding into their work. Other participants felt that while PVOs should insulate their activities from political considerations, they should not hesitate to address the policies of governments and, in this case, paramilitary groups which generate the need for humanitarian aid. One PVO executive said that since questioning whether Contra aid could be humanitarian was really an attack on the Administration's Central America policy, he, for one, supported that policy and saw no inconsistency in calling such aid humanitarian.

The situations in Kampuchea and Central America recalled similar circumstances elsewhere. If actions along the Nicaraguan/Honduran border were somehow inappropriate, should questions not be raised as well about the more broadly supported "humanitarian" assistance provided to the Afghan resistance in and through Pakistan? How did helping the Contras compare with aiding secessionist groups in Northern Ethiopia? Was not the U.S. government's Contra aid strategy similar to its support for anti-government rebels in Mozambique, advancing through some of the same PVO surrogates, under the guise of humanitarian aid, a political and military agenda?

Three discussion groups pursued these issues in more detail. They were chaired by Corinne Johnson, Secretary of the International Division of the American Friends Service Committee, Roger Winter, Director of the U.S. Committee for Refugees, and Don Bjork, Associate Executive Director of World Relief. The plenary adopted the groups' recommendations that the draft InterAction Statement on humanitarian assistance (Appendix I) be further refined, that future discussions be planned using case studies from other countries, and that a checklist of questions be drawn up for use in the decision-making of PVOs and in their manuals for overseas staff.

The Symposium quite clearly generated more questions than answers. However, by illuminating some of the complexities which confront PVOs seeking to function amidst conflict, it raised issues needing attention by today's aid practitioners. It also reflected such extensive interest that the issues were soon placed before the PVO community as a whole.

The 1986 InterAction Forum

The InterAction membership, a larger group than had attended the Symposium, devoted a full day to humanitarian assistance issues at the organization's Annual Forum, held May 18-21 in McAfee, New Jersey. The Forum's general theme was "Building Leadership for Voluntary International Action." The fact that most of the final day had been reserved for humanitarian aid discussions reflected the growing importance attached to the subject. Earlier in the conference the new United Nations High Commissioner for Refugees Jean-Pierre Hocké had delivered a major address on "The Worldwide Status of Refugees and the Impact on Development."

The Forum conversations began where the Symposium had left off. Having struggled with a title which would express urgency without being unduly alarmist, the Working Group had arrived at "Humanitarian Assistance Under Fire." "Today's session," observed Larry Minear in welcoming the hundred participants, "is designed ... to raise fundamental questions about humanitarian aid" and to examine some of the difficulties experienced in providing it. Whereas six months earlier only PVOs had gathered around the table, this occasion involved a high-level government official with humanitarian aid responsibilities and a member of the press who had reviewed recent large-scale aid activities in Africa.

James N. Purcell, Jr., Director of the State Department's Bureau of Refugee Programs, began his keynote address by reviewing recent humanitarian challenges and accomplishments. His praise for the work of PVOs in overseas refugee programs and domestic resettlement has already been noted (page 6). He outlined what he saw as a deepening partnership in meeting refugee needs between PVOs and various United Nations agencies, the U.S. and other governments, and the international Red Cross movement. "Different voluntary agencies,"he observed, "will see different roles for themselves in different situations. Some will carry out their work 'under fire', in situations of military conflict and political tension. Others will concentrate on longer term programs — education, child care, infrastructure improvements, avoiding the conflict situations in which development aid runs up against the political reality of battle lines and contested frontiers."[9]

Aware of PVO concern about the politicization of humanitarian assistance, Purcell challenged the view that the Geneva Conventions and Protocols stand in judgment over current U.S. policies and programs. These instruments, he observed, "establish a minimum level of assistance which must always be permitted. But they do not preclude anyone from providing additional humanitarian aid to one side or the other, beyond the required minimum." Moreover, since the instruments "at no point ... even define the term 'humanitarian assistance,' [they cannot be violated by] the actions of the U.S. Government in providing nonlethal or humanitarian assistance to people involved in political or military conflict situations."[10]

Purcell also took issue with the view that humanitarian assistance must be provided to all in need. "To suggest, as some of you have, that humanitarian aid should only be provided on an equal basis to both sides in a conflict would prevent courageous medical teams from providing life-saving medical aid inside Afghanistan; would eliminate hospitals and medical stations for Afghan refugees in Pakistan; would militate against the surgical wards treating victims of fighting at the Thai-Cambodian border; and would rule out other worthwhile programs throughout the world. In theory, one can agree that all humanitarian aid should be available to both sides; in practice, such a philosophy would prevent major life-sustaining programs in situations throughout the world in which access is available only to one side or the other."[11]

Concerned about increased political activism by PVOs on aid issues, Purcell expressed the view that "As U.S. citizens, all of us have the right to participate in the political process that governs our country and sets direction for government policies at home and abroad. Within that framework, private citizens and organizations have the freedom to support or disagree. But as agencies committed to humanitarian aid, I hope you will concentrate your efforts on programs in which you are prepared to help rather than opposing those with which you may disagree but which others among you are prepared to support." His comment highlighted the diversity of views among PVOs within the InterAction community and beyond.[12]

PVO respondent John Hammock, Executive Director of Oxfam America, took strong exception to Purcell's remarks. The Reagan Administration had launched a major attack on humanitarian assistance, he charged, of which aid to the Contras is the most obvious but by no means the only example. Aid is one element in the Administration's broader political strategy of destabilizing the Nicaraguan government. Its recipients are not civilians; its contents are not for basic human needs; its providers are not impartial. With politics rather than human need controlling, Hammock contended, such aid clearly does not meet the expectations of the Geneva Conventions and Protocols.

In illustration of the extent to which the basic concept of humanitarian assistance had been distorted, Hammock noted that an Oxfam request for a U.S. government license to ship agricultural tools to Nicaragua remained ungranted (even unanswered) two months after submission. Yet the Administration had approved in only four days the request of a recently formed PVO to send a helicopter, ostensibly for medical work, to the Honduran/Nicaraguan border. During the years 1982-84, Oxfam applications for shipments to Vietnam and Kampuchea had also experienced delays and, in four cases of sixteen, rejection. Oxfam's programs had suffered accordingly, Hammock said. He welcomed recent legislative changes making it possible for PVOs to be granted general licenses for shipments to such countries rather than requiring individual licenses for each shipment.[13]

Hammock urged his PVO colleagues to become more actively concerned about government manipulation of the concept of humanitarian assistance and about the impact of U.S. government policies on American PVOs. "If PVOs allow government to politicize humanitarian assistance," he warned, "we will have difficulty distinguishing ourselves from the U.S. government and [will] become tools of U.S. foreign policy." PVOs for their part need to become partisans for the poor overseas, Hammock said, though not supporters of a given government or political party. "Real human beings," he said, are at the core of PVO programs and of humanitarian aid discussions. Conflict with the U.S. government, which has no such overriding orientation, should therefore be expected and accepted.

The third panelist, Josh Friedman, was a reporter whose coverage in the New York newspaper *Newsday* of the 1984-85 African famine had won a Pulitzer Prize. He directed impassioned and strongly negative comments at both the U.S. government and American PVOs for their humanitarian aid activities.

"Global politics play an increasing role in where the U.S. government goes," he observed. During most of 1984, virtually unlimited amounts of U.S. aid had been available for Kenya while Ethiopia, in the grip of far graver food shortages, received nothing. U.S. policy-makers approach human needs in a given country with the view, Friedman said, that "Either you're for us or against us." The needs of the poor are thus held hostage to relationships between governments. Food has been used increasingly as a diplomatic weapon in recent years, he observed. The upsurge in U.S. bilateral aid at the expense of U.S. assistance channeled through the United Nations is one clear indication. The U.S. government has also stepped up aid to and through more fundamentalist American PVOs, forgetting, Friedman said, that "the U.S. public doesn't want food handed out on a Bible."

Hunger and Politics

To respond to starving people is a fundamental expression of our civilization and of our values. We've been willing to respond without regard to politics. As President Reagan has said, "A hungry child knows no politics."

AID Administrator M. Peter McPherson, responding to a question in May 1985 about whether the United States would provide emergency assistance to Ethiopia.

PVOs for their part have been too inattentive to the distorting effects of resources and patronage, Friedman charged. They have become too dependent on the U.S. government for resources, irrespective of the extent to which this limits their humanitarian responsiveness. At the same time, PVO fundraising from the American public has become a spectacle, pitting PVOs against each other and promoting a simplistic approach to complex problems of human suffering and underdevelopment.

Friedman urged greater professionalism within the PVO community both at home and in developing countries. He recommended more joint fund raising, as practiced in Europe, to minimize destructive competitiveness among agencies and to upgrade the content of promotional material. He urged PVOs to establish an auditing agency to augment accountability and public trust and a training entity to enhance the competence of PVO personnel. He concurred with Hammock that more circumspection in the use of government resources was in order.

Following animated discussion of the plenary presentations, the scene shifted to workshops on the Sudan, on South and Southern Africa, and on working with the new governments in Haiti, Uganda, and the Philippines. Once again, background information had been circulated in advance. The presence of PVO personnel with extensive overseas experience lent concreteness and immediacy to the discussions.

Recent events had again propelled the **Sudan** into the public eye. The civil strife and weather conditions which had interfered with food production and created widespread food shortages were also slowing the work of the aid agencies. The number of aid personnel in the South was dwindling in the face of the injury and death experienced by current PVO and U.N. staff. Against this background, sketched by Mark Publow of World Vision and Fred Gregory of World Concern, David Guyer led the group in a discussion of the following issues:

1. How should agencies deal with the tension between the urgent need for assistance and the danger to which aid providers are exposed? Given the nature of the civil strife and the very real hazards posed to relief personnel, should PVOs seek to work out with the authorities understandings within which their operations might proceed? Practically speaking, how could this done when the Sudanese government and the Sudan Peoples' Liberation Front are at war?

2. With the conflict in the South, PVO activities had become concentrated in the North. Were agencies active only in the North meeting their obligations to assist people wherever they are located? Would assisting in one region of the country make an agency unacceptable in the other? Did the vulnerability of staff to conflict in the South

relieve agencies of their obligation to assist there?

3. Since human needs would probably remain largely unmet as long as the civil strife continued, was there a role for PVOs in seeking to bring about an end to the hostilities? Noting that religious organizations had facilitated an end to the previous Sudanese civil war in 1972, participants asked whether PVOs should seek to mobilize world public opinion in that direction. Would doing so create problems in cooperating on relief matters with either side?

4. Should PVOs working in the Sudan approach the central government together? Why not use the good coordination which existed among PVOs in the North to strengthen their hand in dealing with government on aid problems, even granted the government's reluctance to deal with PVOs as a group?

The group concluded that in conflict situations like the Sudan, PVOs should coordinate activities closely among themselves and with the governments on whose consent their continued work depends. PVOs should exercise great caution, however, in approaching the government together, even to obtain fuller government cooperation in their work. To be sure, more agencies were active in the North and more assistance was provided there. However, security problems in the South rather than any PVO partiality to the North justified the disproportionate allocations. Parallels were drawn with the massive aid provided to government-controlled areas of neighboring Ethiopia as compared with the more modest levels in the secessionist areas of Northern Ethiopia.

Equally difficult issues confronted the workshop on **South and Southern Africa**, moderated by Richard Scobie of the Unitarian Universalist Service Committee. David Bonbright of the Ford Foundation, Tom Getman of World Vision United States, and Cathy Makhene of World Vision South Africa served as resource persons.

1. Should the U.S. PVO community establish guidelines for its assistance in South Africa? Since apartheid is clearly wrong, should PVOs provide assistance to South Africans only when it helps dismantle apartheid, or is reaching people in need an overriding consideration, whatever is thereby implied about racist structures? Can PVOs help people in the homelands without endorsing the homelands policy? Given the extremity of the needs in South Africa, how can U.S. PVOs not respond?

2. Should PVOs serve as channels for U.S. government aid to South Africa? Would doing so endorse current U.S. policy or compromise PVO operations in the front-line states or in post-apartheid South Africa? Does providing aid in South Africa obligate PVOs to work for stepped up U.S. government pressure against apartheid? Is it possible for individual agencies do both simultaneously?

3. Since South Africa-supported destabilization campaigns are wreaking havoc on people throughout the region, should PVOs active or seeking to become operational in Mozambique, Angola, and other southern African nations address the policies of the South African and U.S. governments? What bearing, positive or negative, would doing so have on their activities in the region?

The group concluded that since poverty and injustice are the fully intended result of deliberate South African government policies, PVOs should conceive of themselves as human rights as well as humanitarian aid organizations. They should be prepared to engage the South African government on broader issues in pursuit of their aid objectives, even given the risk this might pose to their own programs. PVOs also agreed on the need to function in solidarity and close cooperation with indigenous groups, realizing the dangers of such cooperation for South African agencies and personnel. Because current U.S. policy in South and Southern Africa is generally viewed negatively in the region, the group concluded that American PVOs should not serve as channels for U.S. government aid.[14] Indigenous PVOs should be free to make their own decisions respecting the use of such resources.

A more recent discussion of both the urgent human needs and the political complexities of the situation has become available in *Community Development in South Africa: A Guide for American Donors* by Michael Sinclair. "South Africa's history of racial oppression and black political resistance," he writes, "has created a complex political situation that affects almost every dimension of South African society. . . . Although it is not possible to escape the political dimension, it is possible to gain acceptance among black South Africans through sensitivity to the political aspirations and social needs of blacks." While activities which, in the words of Bishop Desmond Tutu, polish the chains of apartheid will be met with suspicion, Sinclair concludes, PVO efforts will be welcome which identify with "black political liberation by [choosing as partners] institutions that are a legitimate part of the black struggle."[15]

Meeting Urgent Human Needs within Political Struggles

Given the Reagan administration's action of the past seven years — actions that have called for at most minor adjustments to the *status quo* — people inside South Africa are very suspicious of anyone and anything linked to the United States. Black South African reaction to American PVOs is character- ized by hesitation and suspicion. This is not to say that PVOs shouldn't come in, or that South Africans will not recognize good work done by people of goodwill. All I am saying is that private voluntary organizations be sensitive to this perception. Therefore, I would say to American PVOs: "be sure to consult South Africans at every level."

Charles Villa-Vicencio, University of South Africa professor, 1987.

Recent and dramatic changes in the governments of **Haiti, Uganda, and the Philippines** had raised many questions. Resource persons for the workshop, which was moderated by John Swenson of Catholic Relief Services, were Harlan Hobgood of the Freedom from Hunger Founda- tion and Roger Winter of the U.S. Committee for Refugees. Questions included the following:

1. What criteria should guide PVO work under repressive regimes so that in times of conflict or periods of transition to more democratic rule, PVOs are not identified with the old regimes? What is the role of humanitarian assistance when a government is harassing those working for democratic political change?

2. What guidelines would assist a PVO in developing relationships with a new government? Should agencies "plunge in" to assist in the transition, or allow a fluid situation to settle first? In countries of great foreign policy importance to the United States, should American PVOs act assertively or exercise particular caution?

3. Do PVOs have a role in educating Americans to the social and political realities, old and changing, in countries in which they work? Should the Congress be cautioned against its perennial desire to channel U.S. government aid through American PVOs in situations in which repression or corruption exists? Should PVOs be more circumspect in utilizing such aid when the U.S. makes it available?

The group viewed transitions of governments as opportunities to es- tablish good working relationships with new political leadership and as open moments when a new government's human needs agenda may be particularly susceptible to PVO influence. Existing agreements may also be refined and regularized. On the other hand, the group felt that the natural PVO impulse to get on with the task of meeting human needs should be moderated and not allowed to obscure the possibility that other transitions might also follow. The coming to power of new Haitian, Ugandan, and Philippine governments had not removed the vulnerability of aid personnel in those countries.

The InterAction Forum stimulated interest in humanitarian aid issues throughout a wider segment of the PVO community. The discussions did not achieve much consensus either on ground rules for PVO involvement in conflict situations or on the draft InterAction Statement (Appendix I). The Forum did produce a sobering sense of the complexity of the situations in which PVOs work and reinforced a desire among PVOs to seek ways to function more effectively in such situations.

State Department Discussions in 1986

Hearing from James Purcell of the issues raised at the InterAction Forum, Deputy Secretary of State John C. Whitehead expressed interest in continuing the dialogue. When Whitehead had assumed his duties in July 1985 as second in command at the State Department, he already had considerable familiarity with PVOs. As a board member of the International Rescue Committee for thirty years and more recently as its president, he had played a key role in establishing its programs for refugees in Somalia and Pakistan and had visited its projects in Thailand and Hong Kong.

Whitehead originally proposed a relaxed half-day session with Inter-Action on a Saturday in the fall of 1986. Due to other demands on his time, the meeting finally took place on Friday, December 5 and lasted just over an hour. Joining Whitehead were other officials with humanitarian assistance responsibilities: M. Peter McPherson, AID Administrator, Jonathan Moore, State Department Coordinator for Refugee Affairs, and seven others from State and AID.

The InterAction delegation was made up of Nan Borton, InterAction Chair and Executive Director of International Voluntary Services, Karl Zukerman, InterAction Vice Chair and Executive Director of HIAS (the Hebrew Immigrant Aid Society), Peter J. Davies, InterAction President and Chief Executive Officer, and John Sewell, Chair of the InterAction Public Policy Committee and President of the Overseas Development

Council. Also present were John Lapp, Executive Director of the Mennonite Central Committee, Robert DeVecchi, Executive Director of the International Rescue Committee, Richard Carr of World Vision Relief Organization, Larry Minear, and two InterAction staff.

Following discussions at the 1985 Symposium and the 1986 Forum, the issues raised with the Administration had been carefully researched and framed by the InterAction Working Group. They had also been shared in general terms with State Department aides in advance. The delegation itself had met to review the issues and discuss their presentation. The group was cordially received by government officials and the exchange was useful, if not altogether satisfying for either party.

Borton's introduction stressed the heterogeneity of the PVO community and yet the shared concern about difficulties facing humanitarian aid and its PVO providers. That shared concern, she said, provided the common backdrop for whatever particular items individuals in the delegation might raise. Acknowledging the diversity of the community, Whitehead praised PVOs for their work as respected aid providers and as partners with the U.S. government. However important the policy concerns PVOs were raising, the more serious threats to U.S. humanitarian assistance, Whitehead believed, lay in congressional budget-cutting of the Administration's foreign aid request and in the lack of an articulate constituency for foreign assistance.

For their part, PVOs raised a number of issues. Most fundamental was the need for more precision in the government's use of the term humanitarian assistance. PVOs clarified that many did not believe, as Purcell had charged in his May speech, that the U.S. government was prevented by international convention from providing assistance of whatever sort it wished to whomever it might chose whenever it saw fit. Calling such assistance humanitarian, however, did violence to the accepted understanding of the term and to *bona fide* humanitarian assistance itself. (News accounts earlier in the week had reported U.S. shipments of "humanitarian" and military aid reaching the Contras on the same flights.)

Humanitarian Assistance and Communism

Anyone who examines the historical record of communism must conclude that any aid directed at overthrowing communism is humanitarian aid.

Washington Times editorial, 10 May 1985.

A second PVO concern had to do with the need for the U.S. government to employ clear and consistent criteria in selecting PVOs as channels for U.S. humanitarian assistance. The Department of Defense, it was noted, cooperates with PVOs which are not registered with AID. Given the proliferation of both PVOs and U.S. government agencies involved in such aid, mutually agreed upon ground rules for all agencies involved in providing humanitarian assistance become ever more important.

PVOs also urged greater government sensitivity to the vulnerability of U.S. and indigenous PVOs providing aid in conflict situations. While PVOs were highly sought after as partners, cooperation was frequently a matter of greater delicacy for them than the U.S. and other governments acknowledged. The mistaken perception that one PVO was using CIA funds had seriously compromised its integrity and had complicated its ability to find indigenous partners. Also cited was the acquiescence by one U.S. embassy in an attempt by a Central American government to discredit an indigenous PVO seeking to provide humanitarian assistance in a contested area. As humanitarian aid is drawn into political and military conflicts, PVOs observed, the mounting vulnerability of aid workers and programs should concern the U.S. government no less than PVOs.

The need for PVOs to preserve their impartiality in politicized situations remained a difficult one for PVOs to dramatize and for U.S. officials to grasp. As a case in point, officials believed the U.S. had been forthcoming in allowing PVOs to distribute U.S. aid to displaced persons in San Salvador without requiring verification that they had not come from areas where the Salvadoran government's authority was being contested. U.S. PVOs would not be allowed, however, to distribute U.S. government aid to people needing it in contested areas themselves. The meeting also did not explore the extent to which PVOs could provide the sought-after political support for the U.S. foreign aid program and still retain their independence as private organizations.

While most of the issues raised by PVOs dealt with ways in which the government was seen to impede their humanitarian activities, one PVO cited the constructive role which the Administration might now play in facilitating such work. Recent legislative and administrative changes were making it more possible for licenses to be granted promptly for PVO shipments to embargoed countries such as Vietnam and Kampuchea. The State Department was urged to expedite the granting of such requests as expressions of humanitarian concern by the American public rather than making them occasions for communicating U.S.

government views to the governments involved.

Overall, the session provided for an opportunity to explore issues of concern to PVOs and the Administration, though the size of the group and the time available did not allow for extended discussion. Whitehead praised the courageous spirit of PVO personnel and acknowledged the perilous circumstances in which they often function. He requested the AID Administrator to develop a mechanism to foster further dialogue and encouraged PVOs to draft what might become, after discussion within the State Department, official guidance to U.S. embassies incorporating PVO concerns.

Events in 1987

Two events in 1987 broadened the InterAction dialogue further still. The first was a discussion with Dr. Robert Wolthuis, Director of the Office of Humanitarian Assistance of the U.S. Department of Defense (DOD). The occasion was a luncheon on January 29 in Washington, D.C. sponsored by InterAction's Humanitarian Assistance Working Group and attended by representatives of about fifteen PVOs. The second was a March 19 panel discussion, also in Washington, at the International Development Conference on "Providing Humanitarian Assistance in Conflict Situations: New Complexities, Abiding Challenges." The audience included about one hundred persons from development groups, academic institutions, the media, and the interested public.

"What is DOD doing in the humanitarian assistance business?", asked Wolthuis as a starting point for the luncheon discussion. He noted that the Defense Department had a history of assisting in humanitarian crises around the world, a unique capacity for providing emergency materiel and personnel assistance in significant amounts, and, as a result of legislative changes in recent years, substantial statutory and congressional support for expanding the scale and scope of its aid activities.

DOD currently has five areas of involvement. In two respects, it facilitates the work of PVOs: by providing them with excess U.S. government property and by transporting their relief supplies. Since first authorized to do so in 1984, DOD has transported on a space-available basis just over one thousand tons of PVO supplies. After a first-year response to nineteen requests for Central America, the program in 1987, given expanded authority to operate world-wide, filled 102 requests for transport to 22 countries in every region. While most of the first-year shipments were for a relatively new Louisiana-based PVO, Friends of the Americas, several dozen PVOs used DOD transport services in 1987. DOD coordinates the assistance it provides with AID, though PVOs receiving excess property or free transport are not limited to agencies registered with AID.

In the other three areas of DOD involvement, Wolthuis explained, U.S. military personnel themselves are the providers of aid in the form of disaster relief, medical assistance, and civic action activities. Such DOD activities were expanded and made more explicitly part of its mandate through changes legislated in 1986. They are now authorized to be carried out in conjunction with military operations if they promote the security interests of the U.S. and the recipient country, enhance the skills of U.S. troops, and have the Secretary of State's approval. DOD's humanitarian work is undertaken to advance U.S. political and military objectives and is part of a strategy of low-intensity conflict, although clandestine activities, Wolthuis noted, may not be underwritten with such funds.

The discussion was about equally divided between PVO inquiries for more details about cooperative possibilities and policy questions about the appropriateness of DOD's involvement in so-called humanitarian assistance. Could DOD expedite the process of making available excess property to PVOs? It would welcome suggestions for doing so. May DOD transport PVO personnel as well as supplies? No. May PVOs join DOD's medical readiness, or med-ready, exercises which provide basic health services to poor communities? These are limited to DOD personnel. Interested PVOs agreed to join together informally to explore improved and expanded cooperative arrangements with DOD.

On the policy side, some PVOs challenged DOD for having "stolen our term" and included within humanitarian assistance various activities which do not meet established international understandings of such aid. Loose use of the term, they suggested, subjected legitimate humanitarian aid providers, already working in perilous situations, to suspicion and physical danger. While DOD indeed has a tradition of community involvement, would it not be preferable to distinguish *civic action*, which may be appropriate for the U.S. armed forces, from *humanitarian assistance*, which, some PVOs held, is not?

Wolthuis countered that PVOs themselves acknowledge significant unmet need beyond what they are able to reach. DOD has been active in some of the very countries reviewed in the InterAction dialogue such as the Sudan, Pakistan, and Haiti. Is it not in the national interest to have such human need more fully met? In doing so, DOD was operating not in freewheeling fashion but rather in close coordination with AID and with the permission of the American ambassador in each such country. DOD activities to date, Wolthuis said, had also been well coordinated with local government officials. Nor need there be confusion between DOD personnel, which are always uniformed, and PVO staff. In short, while the U.S. government and its defense establishment are not neutral in relation to many countries experiencing conflict, the assistance DOD provides is constructive and can properly be termed humanitarian.

Sharing the Means of Life

Humanitarian assistance is an active expression of mutual responsibility in the human community, a responsibility higher than that to any government, party, or policy. It is the unencumbered sharing the means of life.

Corinne Johnson, The American Friends Service Committee, 1987.

The second 1987 event was more wide-ranging and more public. The four panelists assembled in March at International Development Conference were Jean-Jacques Surbeck of the International Committee of the Red Cross, Lt. Colonel George DeAngelo, Wolthuis' Deputy in DOD's Office of Humanitarian Assistance, John Swenson of Catholic Relief Services, and Don Bjork of World Relief.

In introducing the panel, Larry Minear called attention to the finding that there is more conflict in the world today, with civilians more vulnerable, than ever before. (See feature box on page 41.) At the same time, there are more agencies seeking to assist persons caught up in violence. In addition to established aid providers such as the United Nations, the U.S. State Department, the ICRC, and traditional PVOs, he noted, there are new private organizations and U.S. government agencies, including the Department of Defense. Nevertheless, Minear concluded, "for all of the new complexities and the bewildering array of actors, the basic challenge of providing humanitarian aid remains."

Attention focussed on Minear's basic question: "Why is it more and more difficult to provide humanitarian aid?" Surbeck began by confirming from the experience of the ICRC, whose activities are limited to conflict situations, a "tremendous increase" in the need for such aid. In the period of only a decade, from 1974 to 1984, the number of ICRC staff and delegates, which are entirely Swiss to ensure neutrality, had grown from 357 to 890. ICRC delegations had increased from sixteen countries in 1974 to thirty-six in 1984, with sub-delegations in another sixteen countries. Its budget had more than doubled. The ICRC's growth, Surbeck observed, reflected its effort to respond to a larger number of armed conflicts, most of them non-international in character and many of them more protracted than in earlier years. The ICRC has also noted a marked increase in practices prohibited by international law, such as the mistreatment of civilians, and in the priority which states attach to political and security concerns.

Reality Has Become More Complex

Today, a great number of people are involved in implementing humanitarian law. Among the situational or inherent obstacles to observance, there is the sheer number of rules involved. The inclusion of new actors, such as resistance fighters, partisans and more recently guerilla fighters, as legitimate combatants (with their rights and obligations) should have led to greater observance since these new actors have been granted new responsibilities. But with technical progress on the one hand and the new forms of warfare on the other — in particular the advent of total war — actors have continued to proliferate.

Despite its qualitative improvements, humanitarian law is not close enough to the real world. This is particularly the case for the crucial distinction between civilians and combatants. Reality has become more complex and distinctions more uncertain. Total conflicts with total mobilization of human and economic resources have meant an increasing participation of civilian facilities and of civilians themselves in the war efforts, thus blurring the distinction between civilians and combatants, especially for those responsible for applying humanitarian law. ...

But is there a way to improve the situation? The main one, indeed the radical remedy, would of course be an improvement in the international political climate and the patient and loyal quest on all sides for a new consensus based on greater equity and justice. The violence of a few desperados would then become irrelevant.

Independent Commission on International Humanitarian Issues, Humanitarian Law at a Time of Failing National and International Consensus.

Bjork indicated that World Relief, like all private humanitarian aid agencies, was struggling in highly complex situations with the monumental task of providing impartial and effective aid to those in desperate need. The principles which guide his agency's activities include political neutrality and a willingness to challenge governments at appropriate points. Conversations with the U.S. and host governments were a regular feature of World Relief's work. His organization's services, too, were increasingly in demand.

Swenson explained some of the difficulties Catholic Relief Services had experienced. Although the activities of ICRC-like PVOs are recognized by governments party to the Geneva Conventions, PVOs in actual practice "work at the suffrance of host governments." While PVOs are committed to aid all in need, they seldom "control the contexts in which they operate" and may be limited to providing assistance "on one side of a conflict line." Unable to do everything everywhere, individual PVOs are faced with tough choices, sometimes reaching different decisions about how best to proceed. They can and should, Swenson stated, appeal to governments and to public opinion for fuller access to those in need. However, "the moral argument unfortunately is not always the argument that ends the day."

DeAngelo described, as had Wolthuis in January, the Defense Department's humanitarian assistance-related work, emphasizing both long-time DOD involvement in civic and humanitarian programs and its more recent expansion of activity. He provided several illustrations of DOD in action, stressing its close connection with the State Department and AID. "We're involved purely for humanitarian reasons," he stated, acknowledging at the same time that the aid provided served as a "good deterrent and tool . . . to help keep down insurgencies around the world."

The panelists were challenged at many points. Since the Geneva Conventions divorce humanitarian assistance from extraneous agendas, does aid provided for reasons of religion (in the case of the PVOs) or national security (DOD) qualify as humanitarian? When misery cries out for attention, is it humanitarian to insist on the rigorous application of certain ground rules? Is public confidence not undermined when differences in philosophy and approach lead even well-established PVOs to respond differently to a given crisis? The emergence of a new breed of PVOs with patently political objectives, it was observed, further confuses the situation. Members of the audience also questioned the appropriateness and professionalism of PVO activities in specific countries.

The consensus of the International Development Conference discussion was that while providing humanitarian aid has never been easy, the task has been made vastly more difficult by the complexities in which today's human need is set. Universal principles, however widely acknowledged, require finely tuned application to individual situations, and different aid providers will apply those principles differently. International convention may provide a supportive and protective context in which aid agencies function, but the instruments of the international community are fragile and the activities they seek to protect are easily compromised.

More broadly, the events in the InterAction dialogue during the years 1985-87 suggest that, however exemplary the past activities of PVOs, the abiding challenge of providing humanitarian aid in increasingly complex situations requires a new degree of professionalism. The following chapter analyzes some of the issues that such professionalism will need to address.

CHAPTER III
THE ISSUES

The InterAction discussions described in the previous chapter identified issues which have a critical bearing on the effectiveness of PVOs as humanitarian assistance providers. This chapter analyzes those issues, with particular attention to the areas of consensus and disagreement within the PVO family.

Shared PVO Values and Traditions

One prominent theme of the InterAction dialogue — indeed it was the starting point for the InterAction discussions themselves — was an affirmation of the basic values and traditions of PVOs. "Principles are important to us as agencies," James MacCracken told the 1985 Symposium. In the light of the more complex world in which PVOs are called to assist people in need, he observed, PVOs need to "redefine our principles."

Three essential principles which characterize many PVOs involved in the dialogue emerged from the two-year series of discussions, reinforced by long-standing PVO traditions and by other aspects of PVO life and activities within InterAction.

First and foremost, PVOs are **private.** That is, they are agencies which receive a substantial portion of their resources from non-governmental, private sector contributions. Those resources, which may be augmented by others from governments or United Nations institutions, are used in accordance with ground rules specified by boards of directors composed of private citizens, to whom PVOs are accountable for accomplishing their self-selected objectives.

Second, PVOs are **voluntary.** That is, they are composed of people who associate themselves voluntarily to accomplish certain common objectives. They are an expression of, and seek to cultivate, constituencies of support among persons who share their goals. Their policy-making boards are made up of private citizens who serve without pay.

Third, PVOs are **people-to-people** in orientation. That is, they express the concerns of the American people through direct ties with people in other countries. Many of their programs place a premium on strengthening popular institutions and encouraging local decision-making in developing countries. Many PVOs also stress mutuality, collaborating, for example, in two-way exchanges rather than simply transferring resources from the U.S. to developing countries.

These principles make for an action-oriented, can-do approach. The organizational style of PVOs tends to be non-bureaucratic and decentralized. As many resources as possible are generally committed to programmatic objectives, as few as possible to administrative costs. PVOs as a group have come to be identified with a dedicated and energetic style of engagement at the grass-roots level in developing countries.

As MacCracken suggested, an understanding of PVO history and traditions provides a sound basis for charting an appropriate future course. The new complexities of current humanitarian assistance situations, the International Development Conference discussion concluded, need to be faced in the context of the abiding challenges PVOs have met in the past. The broader international humanitarian effort would hardly be well served were PVOs to desert what over the years they have learned to do best in an effort, for example, to become more like governmental aid providers.

While the InterAction dialogue reaffirmed a common PVO history, the conversations also illustrated the heterogeneity of the PVO community. The 112 member agencies of InterAction include some with annual budgets in excess of $200 million, some with budgets of less than $500,000. Some have programs in scores of countries, others in one or two. Some have been in existence for more than forty years, others were established in this decade. Some have roots in religious communities, others are non-sectarian or secular. Some emphasize charity, others encourage entrepreneurial activities. Some as a matter of principle accept no government funds, others have budgets mostly of government origin. Some operate with partners at the international level and in developing countries, others do not. Some have no overseas programs at all, concentrating on education and advocacy in the U.S.[1]

While such diversity does not make the development of a common approach to humanitarian assistance impossible, it does complicate that task. The failure of broad consensus to emerge on the draft Statement on Humanitarian Assistance (Appendix I) during the two-year period suggests the difficulty of finding meaningful common ground among InterAction's member agencies. The difficulty would be compounded if U.S. PVOs which are not InterAction members were also involved. As of December, 1987 205 U.S. PVOs were registered with AID. Still others are not, making the PVO universe immense indeed. (InterAction's 112 members are listed in Appendix VI.)

While reflecting the pluralism of American society, the diversity of PVOs has less attractive aspects as well. The spectacles of competitiveness and lack of coordination in responding to the African emergency were identified at the 1986 Forum as serious problems. Concern was also expressed throughout the dialogue about the undermining of the credibility of established and reputable PVOs by the activities of other private groups, particularly in Central America. The public opinion poll released in early 1987 also suggested that given a waning (though still significant) public preference for the aid activities of PVOs over those of the U.S. government, PVOs should not rest on their laurels. Clearly, an affirmation of shared values and traditions, including diversity, deserves to provide the basis for charting the future.

Greater Recognition of International Law and Custom

A second major theme of the dialogue was the need for more explicit recognition of the context provided for PVO activities by international law and custom. The presentation at the 1985 Symposium on PVO traditions was followed by one on the rights and responsibilities of PVOs within that international framework. Subsequent discussions throughout the two-year period have underscored the relevance of that framework to PVO activities.

Acknowledging the importance of this broader international context would break new ground for many American PVOs. This is not to say that their international activities over the years have been carried out wholly without reference to international law and custom. They have been more preoccupied for the most part, however, with the laws of the United States and of individual developing countries as these affect their operational activities. Respondents to the InterAction questionnaire indicated that many agencies do not have at their disposal the expertise they would like in this area.

While greater attention to international law and custom may thus be overdue, their application to the day-to-day activities of PVOs in conflict situations is frequently anything but self-evident. The ICRC representative noted at the 1985 Symposium that the Geneva Conventions and Protocols recognize and seek to protect the role of the ICRC and other impartial, non-governmental humanitarian assistance organizations. For the most part, however, they do not provide clear-cut definitions of humanitarian assistance or lend themselves to ready application. A recent effort to produce a guidebook applying international law and custom to the operational activities of PVOs confirms how complex that process can prove.[2]

The problem appears to be less the myopia of American PVOs than the complexities of international law itself. "One of the reasons why humanitarian norms are not always observed," notes the Independent Commission on International Humanitarian Issues, "is the complex or even esoteric character of the rules." The fundamental principles at present are "drowned" in myriad operational principles.[3]

International humanitarian law, it seems, is both overly detailed and not detailed enough. As the world's population has increased from one billion to five billion, the ten articles in the original Geneva Convention of 1864 have grown to six hundred. Even these, however, do not address humanitarian issues in all situations, particularly those involving disturbances and conflicts within nations which have become so numerous of late. Those who have pressed for a set of streamlined principles applicable in all circumstances have encountered the objection that *more* rather than *less* detail is required if the application of basic principles is to be incontrovertible.

While international legal expertise may not have been essential in an earlier and simpler day and while the application of international law and custom to the daily activities of PVOs is difficult, the InterAction discussions make clear that understanding such provisions can have a direct bearing on the execution and outcome of humanitarian activities today. The importance of the rule that refugee camps be located at least fifty kilometers from borders, for example, was confirmed by the consequences of ignoring it. The opening of new programs in Honduras closer to the Nicaraguan border, attracting Nicaraguan refugees from established and safer camps, appears to have contributed to the treatment of the refugees from a political and military standpoint.

Good-faith efforts to apply international convention to PVO activities, however important, are not assured of success. Relief workers who had sought to function apolitically have lost life and limb in countries whose governments were bound by international law to provide them protection and access. Agencies seeking to assist in some conflicts have been

requested to leave the areas and even the countries involved. PVOs working in areas controlled by the Sudan People's Liberation Army have been requested by the Sudan government to leave the country altogether, although they have appealed the government's decision.

Conflict and Cooperation in the Southern Sudan

On September 8, 1986 executives of eight U.S. PVOs and religious organizations wrote Secretary of State George Shultz to express their concern for the worsening food situation in the Sudan and "to enlist the more creative involvement of the U.S. government in helping to find solutions to the problems of civil strife and hunger there."

The State Department, replying in a letter dated 16 October 1986, indicated that the Department shared "both your concern about the human crisis in southern Sudan and your assessment that the civil war is central to that crisis." After recapping the assistance the U.S. government was prepared to provide "as soon as security permits," the Department stated, "We are willing to cooperate with all neutral, competent relief organizations that can ensure our aid will not be used to support combatants."

State Department letter of 16 October 1986 to the Mennonite Central Committee.

The InterAction dialogue produced examples of the indispensable role of PVOs which, difficulties notwithstanding, have operated with professionalism. Particularly in conflict areas such as Kampuchea and Northern Ethiopia, their ability to transcend political divisions was seen as positioning them to make unique contributions. In "zones of political and military conflict," one review concludes, "voluntary relief agencies . . . may have a special opportunity to be of service. If they abide by their professed standards of meeting emergency human needs, by whatever principled and practical means possible, they are able and willing to take risks to reach people who would otherwise be defined as beyond the pale of governments vying for political advantage."[4]

The draft InterAction Statement (Appendix I) moves in the direction of affirming the relevance of international law and custom to U.S. PVO activities. Citing the Geneva Conventions and Protocols, it notes that humanitarian aid is expected to be "offered impartially . . . and strictly on the basis of need, free from extraneous objectives and managed by entities which can assure its efficiency." The InterAction discussions, however, have left none of these elements unchallenged. Participants repeatedly questioned what is meant by impartiality, how realistic it is to expect extraneous objectives to be excluded, and why aid providers should be limited to experienced agencies of proven effectiveness. Questions such as these may help explain the lack of broader endorsement of the draft InterAction Statement.

The concept of impartiality proved at one and the same time most central and most perplexing.

- Are PVOs impartial when they aid Kampucheans in Thailand but not in Kampuchea, Afghans in Pakistan but not in Afghanistan, Nicaraguans in Honduras but not in Nicaragua? If impartiality requires helping people in need on all sides of a conflict or not helping at all, isn't impartiality the enemy of pragmatic humanitarianism?

- Does simply offering assistance to persons on warring sides meet a PVO's obligation, or must a PVO do more, even to the extent of risking program resources and staff? Should there be a rough proportionality to need in the aid provided on opposing sides of a conflict? How might this be achieved?

- When those needing humanitarian aid are caught up in compelling political struggles, such as that of South African blacks against apartheid, can such aid be impartial? Indeed, should it not also, or instead, be an instrument for their liberation?

- Can assistance by a super-power to those suffering on one side of a conflict be considered impartial? When channeled through PVOs, does such aid become impartial, or at least more impartial?

Continued PVO wrestling with the nature of impartiality and its bearing on PVO activities is clearly needed. While many PVOs welcome the recognition and protections afforded by the Geneva Conventions and Protocols and international law, the precise nature of the resulting obligations requires additional attention.

The InterAction dialogue has illustrated not only the importance of international legal safeguards but also their fragility. This was reflected in the InterAction delegation's request of government officials that the U.S. use the term "humanitarian assistance" with more precision and be more sensitive to politicizing the work of U.S. and indigenous PVOs.

The tenuous attention of governments to their own obligations was also apparent in discussions of the various conflict situations. PVOs have experienced difficulties in gaining access to people in contested areas such as the Southern Sudan and Northern Ethiopia, El Salvador and Sri Lanka. Even U.N. authorities have been denied access to Kampuchean refugees in camps along the Thai border.

U.S. PVOs would benefit, the discussions suggest, from connecting more effectively with the global community of active concern about humanitarian issues. A late 1988 conference on humanitarian assistance co-sponsored by the International Council of Voluntary Agencies and the Henry Dunant Institute of the international Red Cross movement will provide a setting for reviewing issues related to the status and security of humanitarian assistance organizations in conflict and non-conflict situations. The InterAction dialogue also suggested the value in certain situations of transferring operational responsibilities from U.S. PVOs to international or indigenous partner agencies.

Greater Attention by PVOs to Matters Political

American PVOs have traditionally prided themselves on keeping themselves divorced from politics. In fact, one major element in their attractiveness to private contributors has been the general perception that they have steered clear of political entanglements and are reaching needy people directly — that is, apolitically. While the public opinion poll described in Chapter I indicated that popular American perceptions may now be finding less to distinguish PVO aid from government assistance, the survey also found that people associate private assistance with humanitarian objectives while viewing government aid as more political in character.

Americans, by and large, view helping people as an activity set in a political vacuum, an approach which differentiates them somewhat from Europeans. Many Americans consider the best PVOs those which have the least to do with governments. One of the recurring themes of the InterAction dialogue — that PVOs need to become far more attentive to the political contexts in which they seek to provide such aid — would thus require major changes in the ways PVOs approach their work and present themselves to the public.

The InterAction dialogue suggests that the complexities of the situations in which PVOs are involved limit the extent to which their activities can be actually be divorced from governments. Rather than minimizing the political dimensions of their activities, PVOs are sensing the need to become more fully aware of them. The discussions suggest that PVOs should preserve the best of their traditions of apolitical aid while at the same time becoming more politically astute. The InterAction conversations bear out the observation of the Independent Commission that "In order to be really useful, a 'humanitarian strategy' must take the political environment into account."[5] This would appear to be true at the level of individual countries, developed and developing, and at the international level as well.

In actual fact, PVOs as aid providers cross paths with governments at many points. They gain access to developing countries only after signing agreements with those governments which specify the ground rules for the entry of relief supplies, personnel, and personal effects. Once operational, PVOs develop relationships with officials at various levels from local to national. Three-quarters of the PVOs responding to the 1985 InterAction survey reported working with the governments of developing countries. The connections are numerous.

American PVOs also interact in countless ways with the U.S. government. PVOs which negotiate grants and contracts with the U.S. government must be registered with AID, to which they are strictly accountable. Seventeen of the twenty survey respondents reported working with AID, ten with the State Department. Even PVOs not accepting U.S. government resources are bound by government rules and regulations which, for example, impose restrictions on PVO travel to, and activities in, embargoed countries. PVOs are also subject to U.S. laws respecting tax deductibility of contributions to, and postal rates of, non-profit organizations. PVOs must be recognized by the Internal Revenue Service to receive such contributions. Some PVOs also engage in education and fund-raising activities which involve state and local authorities.

Although PVOs today have not forsaken their private and non-governmental traditions, their conventional emphasis on their distance from governments may require review. In routine relief and development activities, PVOs interact more frequently with governments than is generally realized. In conflict situations, the case studies indicated, those routine interactions are charged with particular sensitivity and importance. The ability of PVOs to manage those interactions, the discussions suggest, have a major bearing on their success as humanitarian aid practitioners. PVOs are finding the need to engage governments *more* rather than *less*, even though, as one panelist told the International Development Conference group, "the moral argument unfortunately is not always the argument that ends the day."

The InterAction process has produced a general awareness of the importance of a new realism among PVOs about the legitimately political dimensions of their activities. Indeed, such a realism may be a prerequisite for developing the political wisdom needed to function effectively. Very little consensus emerged from the dialogue, however, on many basic aspects of the tension between retaining a fundamentally apolitical approach to humanitarian assistance and managing increasingly critical relations with governments. Areas which stand in need of further attention include the following.

1. To what extent can and should humanitarian assistance be divorced from the political agendas of governments?

Some InterAction members believe that the divorce can and should be complete. Humanitarian aid, they hold, should be provided because people are in need, not to assist (or embarrass) governments or win hearts and minds, not to gain strategic advantage for the United States or stanch (or fan) the fires of social or political discontent.

Identifying the American people and their government with helping people, the reasoning goes, will have long-term rewards for the United States. If such are the results of providing aid, well and good — but they should not be the controlling rationale for doing so. As people-to-people agencies, PVOs should not be forced to carry short-term foreign policy messages on behalf of the U.S. government. Impartiality as envisioned in the Geneva Conventions is not only possible; it is also indispensable.

Other InterAction members hold with equal conviction that it is neither possible nor desirable for the aid which PVOs provide, whether of private or U.S. government origin, to be divorced from U.S. foreign policy agendas. American PVOs are, after all, American. They should not be expected to disguise or downplay their identity and roots. Expectations of impartiality should be tempered by an awareness that people suffer these days in a world dominated by governments and ideologies.

The ability of PVOs to make wise compromises, the reasoning goes, is the test of effective humanitarian action. From this perspective, charges one critic, the draft InterAction Statement (Appendix I) ignores the reality that "large-scale humanitarianism today inevitably includes a governmental component, complete with attendant matters of national interest. . . . Humanitarian realism requires simultaneous attention to what is morally good and what is politically useful."[6]

Principles of Humanitarian Assistance

The provision of aid to displaced persons must follow certain guiding principles. They are:

1. The legitimate security concerns of displaced persons must be recognized at all times. All assistance programs must recognize that humanitarian actions may create situations of increased vulnerability for the displaced persons, for relief workers and for the local institutions that may be supporting or providing sanctuary to those persons. Therefore, the overriding principle of all humanitarian assistance must be the recognition that ultimate accountability is to the displaced persons and not to the government, the donors or other benefactors of the humanitarian assistance programs.

2. All humanitarian activities should be strictly separated from military and security actions, plans and programs.

3. There should be strict observance of impartiality in the disbursement of aid to non-combatants regardless of political affiliation, location of residence and/or ethnic origin.

4. Assistance must be disbursed on the basis of need.

5. All relocation must be strictly on a voluntary basis, and organizations participating in the relocation of displaced persons must accept verification by a recognized third party neutral of the displaced persons' willingness to voluntarily resettle.

6. Humanitarian assistance, especially food, should be delivered to displaced persons where they are located and should not be used as an inducement to encourage displaced persons to participate in relocation programs or in political, military or other activities that may put them in a zone of conflict.

7. Non-governmental relief organizations which work with displaced persons, whether those persons are registered or non-registered with the appropriate government authorities, must be free from intimidation by the military, policy or other security forces of either party in the conflict. . . .

U.S.AID, *Displaced Persons in El Salvador: An Assessment*, 1984.

The tension felt within the PVO community between isolating aid activities from, and capitalizing on their connection to, the political agendas of governments is illustrated by the situation of displaced persons in Central America. A 1984 AID *Report on Displaced Persons in El Salvador* recommended that all humanitarian activities be strictly separated from military and security actions, plans, and programs and that assistance be disbursed solely on the basis of need.[7] (See feature box on page 53.) On the other hand, State Department officials explained to the InterAction delegation that humanitarian aid provided by the U.S. government to El Salvador, either directly or through PVOs, would not be allowed into contested areas, however critical the need. Within the PVO community, too, support for the principles recommended in the AID report exists in tension with acceptance of what is, in some settings, current U.S. government practice.

2. In an era of heightened East-West conflict, to what extent can U.S. PVOs serve as channels for U.S. government humanitarian assistance and yet retain their impartiality?

Here again there is little consensus. Some InterAction members refuse to accept any and all U.S. government resources, fearing that to do so will make them extensions of U.S. foreign policy. Other InterAction members place few limits on such resources, reasoning that they are provided by the Congress on behalf of the American people to accomplish basic human needs objectives. They believe that as experienced private agencies of acknowledged expertise, PVOs can help assure that such resources are well utilized. Still other PVOs accept government resources on a case-by-case, country-by-country basis.

The InterAction dialogue suggests that acceptance by PVOs of U.S. government resources is only one among several linkages of PVOs to U.S. foreign policy. Even PVOs which accept no such resources are subject to certain U.S. government restrictions. Their need for licenses to export aid items to certain countries exposes their humanitarian activities to governmental regulation and, in some cases, interference. At the InterAction Forum and in the meeting with State Department officials, some PVOs expressed their view that the U.S. government should find other ways and means to communicate its intentions toward governments such as Vietnam and Cuba than by denying — or, for that matter, approving — the license applications of people-to-people agencies. Other PVOs find the injection of East-West factors into relations between the U.S. government and American PVOs unavoidable and even appropriate.

With or without U.S. Government resources, American PVOs are sensing the need to be more aware of how their American origin affects their ability to function in conflict settings. At several points the InterAction dialogue suggested that U.S. PVOs, simply by virtue of being American, may carry political baggage which, like it or not, complicates their task. What was observed by South Africans of American visitors may apply to Americans elsewhere as well, that "Americans either spend a great deal of time defending the Reagan administration's [foreign] policy or attempting to dissociate themselves from it."[8]

Once again, there are differences among U.S. PVOs in how they view the bearing of their American identity on their aid activities. Some have indicated that in certain conflicts to which the U.S. is party, they will be active only through international colleague agencies. Some have underscored the need for the U.S. government to avoid using PVOs for intelligence-gathering purposes. Others sense less of a problem. In the words of one executive director, "We are not impartial. We are a one hundred percent American organization. We believe in freedom, democracy, and human rights. We fly the American flag, contrary to what most international organizations do. We are definitely not neutral."[9]

In recent years, the question of establishing a ceiling on the amount of U.S. government resources a given PVO may accept has been a recurring item of debate. Current law requires that a U.S. PVO receive no more than eighty percent of its international budget (excluding food assistance and excess property) from the U.S. government. Various proposals under discussion would lower the maximum federal share allowable over a period of years. Whatever the percentages, discussions of PVO "privateness" have generally not examined the connections between acceptance of federal funds and independence from U.S. foreign policy. The InterAction dialogue suggests that the linkage is worth reviewing.

3. To what extent can PVOs accept U.S. government resources and take independent positions regarding U.S. policies?

The InterAction State Department visit illustrates the issue. On the one hand, InterAction pressed for the visit and received a fair hearing for its views. Such a meeting would probably not have taken place at all were the PVOs not viewed as partners with the U.S. government, utilizers of its funds, and implementors of its policies and interests. In the context which their partnership with the government provided, however, PVOs had considerable difficulty asserting their policy concerns about humanitarian aid.

Whereas there is now general acceptance among PVOs of the need for exercising more assertiveness in relation to governments, the nature of such assertiveness is less self-evident. Many PVOs now agree, for example, that engaging high-level government officials in dialogue is appropriate. Each InterAction encounter with government, however, highlighted differences among PVOs regarding what the views expressed should be. PVOs hold divergent views about cooperation with the State Department in countries of overriding strategic importance to the United States and with AID in countries where AID missions bar the use of government resources in contested areas. How should the PVO community engage the Defense Department when some PVOs believe that DOD activities are by definition not humanitarian and others seek participation in DOD missions and increased DOD transport for PVO relief supplies?

PVOs also get conflicting advice regarding the content of their advocacy. As James Purcell indicated at the 1986 Forum, the Administration encourages PVO advocacy in support of its policies but asks that when PVOs cannot provide support, they at least refrain from generating opposition. The Congress, too, invites PVO testimony and welcomes PVO involvement, but often in support of strategies in which human needs concerns are not controlling. The variety of PVO viewpoints expressed throughout the two-year InterAction dialogue underscores the difficulties PVOs face in agreeing on common content for their policy dialogue with governments.

4. To what extent should PVOs address broader foreign policy questions?

The InterAction community is also somewhat divided about the extent to which PVOs should use their access to public officials to raise questions about policies and programs beyond those in which they themselves are involved. While PVOs have generally been advocates for those government programs they help administer, many have been more reluctant, as a community as well as individually, to address broader policy issues. One particularly troubling issue has been the extent to which PVOs should speak to matters of security assistance (both military and political/economic aid), which in the Eighties has come to command more than two-thirds of total annual U.S. foreign aid resources.

The InterAction discussions have dramatized that the current world-wide need for humanitarian assistance far outruns the capacity of American PVOs. PVOs frequently work side-by-side with the staffs of U.N. High Commissioner for Refugees, the UN Disaster Relief Organization, UNICEF, AID, and the State Department. However, becoming advocates for the work of U.N. agencies and of governments does not necessary follow from recognizing its importance. Should PVOs, as a dimension of their commitment to assist the poor, work to support — and, where necessary, to change — such activities and policies?

To date, InterAction has engaged in public policy advocacy for human needs policies and programs broadly conceived. One of its priorities for 1987 was to support U.S. funding for international human needs programs, multilateral as well as bilateral. One of the 1988 objectives of its Public Policy Committee is "to foster debate during the 1988 Presidential elections . . . regarding U.S. policies and principles in relation to the developing world so that U.S. policy in the next administration will be more responsive to development and humanitarian concerns." InterAction will also press for reform of the U.S. foreign aid program and passage of legislation to speed reconstruction and development in sub-Saharan Africa.[10] InterAction's Migration and Refugee Committee has a strong record of successful advocacy for higher levels of U.S. government funding for refugee programs.

The emerging consensus seems to be that PVO advocacy should range beyond assuring resources for programs which PVOs themselves manage. More problematic, the InterAction dialogue demonstrated, is the task of addressing U.S. policy in specific regions such as Central America or the Horn of Africa. Moreover, as U.S. government resources become more scarce, the traditional instincts of PVOs to be advocates first and foremost for their own programs may be reinforced.

The effort by PVOs to pay greater attention to political matters promises to be a long-term challenge. The InterAction dialogue to date has produced general agreement on the need for PVOs to become more knowledgeable about the political settings in which they work. At the same time, the process has raised fundamental questions about how PVOs should approach their dealings with the U.S. and other governments. While there seems to be broad agreement among PVOs about the need to become more politically astute, the nature and content of PVO involvement in the political realm will require further discussion.

Greater Attention by Governments to Matters Humanitarian

Throughout the InterAction process, a companion theme to the need for greater political wisdom among U.S. PVOs has been the need for governments to show greater sensitivity to humanitarian concerns. The discussions understandably devoted major attention to the U.S. government in this context, although other governments came in for attention as well. Most PVOs agree on the urgency for greater sensitivity on the part of governments in areas such as the following, though with certain differences of emphasis or approach.

1. Greater fidelity to the concept of humanitarian assistance.

One of the themes of the InterAction discussions has been that the integrity of humanitarian assistance and of the agencies which provide it could be enhanced by greater care and precision in the use of the term, by governments as well as by PVOs. PVOs responding to the 1985 InterAction questionnaire placed this item at the top of their agendas. Perhaps the most controversial use of the concept was the Administration's request for humanitarian assistance for the Contras. However, InterAction meetings with State and Defense Department officials flagged a number of other problematic uses of the term as well.

The InterAction process also demonstrated a certain disarray among the government agencies and officials with interests in such aid. Within the State Department, they include the Bureau of Refugee Programs, the Bureau of Human Rights and Humanitarian Affairs, regional bureaus and country desks, and special entities such as the Nicaraguan Office of Humanitarian Assistance. Within the State Department is also AID, whose Office on Foreign Disaster Assistance, regional bureaus, and country desks are actively involved. Other interested agencies outside of State with interests in humanitarian assistance include the National Security Council, the Central Intelligence Agency, the Defense Department, and the White House. Even the Department of Transportation sought to get involved in the last African famine.

The diversity of governmental players makes for problems of coordination as well as of definition. InterAction experienced considerable difficulty at various points in identifying someone who could speak authoritatively for the U.S. government on basic humanitarian assistance policy issues. The legislation requesting the expanded role in humanitarian assistance granted the Defense Department, while the subject of interagency discussions, was apparently forwarded to Capitol Hill without the full agreement of other agencies. There would seem to be room for more effective coordination within the government on humanitarian assistance issues.

The Rights of Refugees and the Responsibilities of Governments

The burden of large numbers of refugees weighs heavily on asylum countries in the developing world, and on us all — first and foremost, on the refugees themselves. In our frustration and seeming powerlessness to effect solutions in our own national interests, we [governments] sometimes take actions unworthy of members of a humane international community. The numerous violations of refugees' rights are a depressing commentary on the current state of protection, particularly when they are not met with effective international response. . . .

We reiterate our government's abhorrence of all violations of the rights of refugees, but particularly of forced repatriation, which denies the most basic protection need of refugees. . . . It is tragic that refugees have been forced "home" against their will and without assurances that they will not face persecution on their return, especially when such violations are committed by or with the concurrence of states party to international instruments prohibiting such acts.

The threat to a country of influxes of economic migrants should not be an excuse for refusing asylum or for involuntarily returning home refugees. We join like-minded delegations in calling upon all nations to live up to international standards for the humanitarian treatment of refugees. The international community must also bring its weight to bear on those countries wherein persist the conditions of violence and persecution that perpetuate refugee flows.

U.S. Coordinator for Refugee Affairs Jonathan Moore, addressing the Executive Committee of the U.N. High Commissioner for Refugees, Oct. 6, 1987.

One example of inconsistencies in the U.S. government approach to humanitarian assistance emerges from differences in U.S. policy among various regions. The State Department indicated in the fall of 1986 to PVOs concerned about stepping up such aid to the Southern Sudan that "We are willing to cooperate with all neutral, competent relief organizations that can ensure our aid will not be used to support combatants."[11] (See feature box on page 48.) Had this policy been followed in Central America, some participants in the InterAction discussions felt, the integrity of U.S. humanitarian aid and PVO activities would not have been so seriously compromised.

The PVO effort to encourage greater clarity in the government's use of the concept of humanitarian assistance has had mixed results. James Purcell was doubtless accurate in observing that the Geneva Conventions and Protocols do not prohibit a government from providing any kind of assistance it chooses to anybody in a conflict situation. Many, however, would question his conclusion: that since the Conventions do not define humanitarian assistance, they cannot be violated by "the actions of the U.S. Government in providing nonlethal or humanitarian assistance to people involved in political or military conflict situations." Aid called humanitarian, the InterAction discussions suggest, needs to be consistent with accepted international usage of the term.

2. Clearer recognition by governments of the non-governmental character of PVOs.

The InterAction discussions demonstrated the importance of the retention by PVOs active in conflict situations of their private, non-governmental character. Treatment of PVOs by governments as surrogates for or extensions of government policy was seen to compromise their integrity and therefore undermine their effectiveness.

Both the executive and legislative branches of the U.S. government frequently use PVOs to send messages to other governments. U.S. officials recognize that PVOs can function well in situations in which U.S. government involvement may be inappropriate, impolitic, or unwelcome. The InterAction discussions suggest, however, particularly with reference to South Africa and Central America, that transmitting short-term foreign policy messages may undercut the integrity of PVO programs and the security of their personnel, as would also their use (or the perception of their use) for intelligence gathering. Many PVOs are comfortable, on the other hand, with the concept that their work conveys a longer term message, which may itself also have certain durable foreign policy benefits for the United States: that Americans wish to help people who are suffering.

The InterAction conversations also suggest that governments of developing countries, too, need to avoid using PVOs as extensions of themselves. While serving in that capacity may have some advantages for PVOs, it may also mean that PVOs will not be allowed to function in areas where the host government is not present. The discussions provided a number of examples from Central America and the Sudan in which governments which had welcomed help from PVOs in extending their outreach then turned against PVOs which, in their view, had moved into areas where the government preferred not to be involved. Inappropriately close relations may also create difficulties when governments change, as the PVO experience in Haiti demonstrated. In dealing with the governments of developing countries faced with conflict situations, PVOs face a continuing challenge in finding and protecting the necessary space in which to operate with integrity.

PVOs may wittingly or unwittingly have encouraged their utilization as government extensions. PVOs participated in and welcomed the development of AID policy, adopted in 1982, which recognizes them as partners of the U.S. government and as intermediaries of its policies and programs.[12] (The companion recognition of PVOs as independent agencies in their own right has commanded far less U.S. government attention and a dwindling share of government resources.) While current law now requires that no more than eighty percent of a PVO's international program budget originate with the U.S. government, government officials have been no more concerned than many PVOs about the extent to which substantial government resources, even short of the ceiling, may affect the non-governmental character of PVOs operating where important U.S. interests are at stake.

3. Greater awareness of PVO exposure in conflict situations.

The InterAction dialogue abounds in examples of the fallout of conflicts on PVO programs. Military action by secessionist groups in Northern Ethiopia claimed the lives in 1985 of two Ethiopian nurses employed by World Vision. Persons connected with private relief activities were aboard an aircraft shot down by the Sudan Peoples Liberation Army in the spring of 1986. An aid official was among the U.S. hostages in Lebanon. More than a dozen expatriate aid workers were killed in Nicaragua in 1985-87, along with scores of Nicaraguan human services personnel. Casualties have abounded in other conflict settings as well.

While there had been loss of life among aid personnel in earlier years, the new element in the recent violence has been the singling out of such persons for targeted violence. The consequences, the dialogue suggests, have been profound. Aid programs have not only lost the services of staff. They have themselves become caught up in the encircling tension and violence, the victims of which they had sought to assist.

It would be erroneous to allege that government action has killed such persons. Governments, however, have contributed to an atmosphere permissive of and therefore conducive to such attacks. The same governments which have been involved in the drafting and ratification of international humanitarian safeguards nevertheless, when under pressure, sometimes interpret their agreed upon obligations narrowly and unilaterally. "In the confrontation between power and law," observes the ICRC President Cornelio Sommaruga, "respect for humanitarian principles is too often subject to considerations of State sovereignty."[13]

"In the worsening international climate," his predecessor Alexandre Hay stated, "there is a growing tendency to resort to force, both between and within States, increasing the number of conflicts as well as the number of victims. Confronted with the present crises, governments are tempted to think only in the short term, to reject everything that does not fit in with immediate interests, and to relegate humanitarian considerations to second place behind what they consider to be the imperatives of politics and security. This refusal to implement international humanitarian law defies the whole international community... and inflicts intolerable suffering on the victims of conflicts."[14]

Governments have a role to play in influencing this climate, the Inter-Action dialogue suggests. At issue are government policies which define security narrowly and which fail to address the root causes of violence. Greater attention by governments to the exposure of aid agencies and aid personnel in conflict situations is also linked to larger issues such as the need for rekindling respect for international law and human rights. More broadly still, issues of arms transfer policies and alternative means of problem-solving may also be involved. The linkage of U.S. humanitarian assistance to a strategy of low-intensity conflict may warrant review in this context as well.

Concern among U.S. officials about the growing exposure of U.S. diplomats abroad should make for greater sensitivity to the vulnerability of PVO personnel. The American Foreign Service Association reports "a tremendous acceleration in danger to Americans overseas, particularly to those related to the U.S. government." Two plaques in the State Department lobby honor U.S. diplomats who lost their lives "under heroic circumstances" in the line of duty. The first covers almost two centuries, from 1780 to 1967, when some eighty foreign service officers were lost at sea, killed in earthquakes, and died from smallpox, malaria, and other diseases. The second plaque, covering only the last twenty years, recognizes roughly the same number of diplomats, most of whose deaths, an Association spokesman points out, were by "human agency."[15]

Towards a Humanitarian Spirit in Politics

The main questions I would like to put to you today are these: how should one go about stimulating awareness of humanitarian values among political leaders? How should one foster the humanitarian spirit in politics? How can one demonstrate that in every political situation there are humanitarian aspects which one ignores at one's peril?

We [from the International Committee of the Red Cross], who are every day confronted with the victims' plight, would be grateful should you be able, with your command of political affairs, to conceive of ways and means to promote the acceptance and application of humanitarian law and its principles among political leaders and to bring awareness to public opinion.

With your experience and standing, you have access to most political leaders and you can urge:

a) the speedy ratification of the Additional Protocols [to the Geneva Conventions], which are a basic supplement to humanitarian law in its main areas such as the protection of civilians against hostilities;

b) a better knowledge of the existing instruments of humanitarian law;

c) the faithful application of these instruments in all circumstances, and full cooperation with existing humanitarian organizations;

d) a better use of the institutions and procedures provided for in existing statutory law . . .

The ideal would evidently be to reach the state where humanitarian principles would be so much a matter of course that there would be no need for humanitarian institutions or law. But we are still a long way from achieving this.

Alexandre Hay, President of the International Committee of the Red Cross, addressing the Independent Commission on International Humanitarian Issues, November 1983.

4. Augmented support for enhanced professionalism among PVOs.

The InterAction dialogue has been a means by which PVOs have moved to enhance their "effectiveness and professionalism as providers of humanitarian aid," as the draft Statement on Humanitarian Assistance (Appendix I) puts it. Several roles have emerged for governments, again with the focus on the U.S. government, in assisting PVO efforts in this area.

The U.S. government over the past fifteen years has made a sizeable contribution to enhancing the professionalism of PVOs. AID made grants through most of the Seventies of more than $10 million annually to enhance PVO management capacity for carrying out international development programs. These grants were followed in the Eighties by at least twice that amount annually to improve the delivery of PVO field programs themselves. Better PVO program planning and evaluation have resulted. AID officials credit PVOs with having become both more sophisticated about the policy environments in which they operate and more savvy about the political contexts, at home and abroad, in which their programs are set. The U.S. government plans to continue its strengthening of PVOs in this area.

The U.S. government could also enhance PVO professionalism by avoiding a "divide and conquer" approach to the PVO community. The charge made at the InterAction Forum that the Reagan Administration is seeking out conservative religious PVOs to implement its foreign policy was not further examined during the dialogue. The U.S. government representative on the same occasion, however, did confirm its intention to seek out those PVOs which "are prepared to support" particular programs to which other PVOs object.

It may be quite natural for a given Administration to develop working partnerships with PVOs with which it feels particularly comfortable. However, when the government plays off some PVOs against others, it does not contribute to greater PVO effectiveness or enhance the professionalism of the community as a whole. Again, substantial U.S. national interests are served — and those of other nations as well — when the U.S. government resists the understandable temptation in dealing with PVOs to "relegate humanitarian considerations to second place behind . . . the imperatives of politics and security."[16]

Governments will naturally be more willing to respect and enhance the integrity of PVOs to the extent that PVOs themselves are working to protect and augment their own integrity. PVOs operating with very political agendas themselves, particularly when those agendas diverge from those of governments, will be hard-pressed to argue that governments should forswear injecting political considerations into humanitarian assistance activities. If PVOs are scrupulously apolitical themselves, they are in a better position to seek the forbearance of governments from politicizing their work.

The InterAction discussions thus challenge PVOs not only to become more conscious of the political dimensions of their activities but also, through ongoing advocacy efforts, to help create and protect in their relations with governments the space necessary for their own apolitical activities to succeed.

Toward Greater Professionalism among PVOs

Perhaps the most frequently recurring theme of the InterAction discussions has been the complexity of the issues involved. The description by the International Committee of the Red Cross official at the 1985 Symposium of his agency's work could be writ large for all humanitarian aid providers. "Few situations are entirely black and white," he observed. "There are many shades of gray, [and it is these] in which we navigate." The experience of many PVOs corroborates the consensus of the International Development Conference panel that PVOs must continually seek to apply their principles to highly complex and changing situations. It would be naive for PVOs to expect their principles to be routinely respected by governments which frequently see themselves as locked in life-and-death struggles.

Complexity characterized every step of the InterAction process, from the preliminary conversations in early 1985 to the more recent developments in 1987, from the detailed planning sessions of the Humanitarian Assistance Working Group to the high-level meeting with senior State Department officials. While the discussions identified the qualities inherent in humanitarian assistance, they produced no body of knowledge which lends itself to universal application, no unanimous statement on humanitarian assistance, not even a straightforward definition from international or U.S. law to guide aid practitioners in highly individualized conflicts.

Coming to terms with such complexity demands a professionalism of PVOs far beyond that of earlier days, as James MacCracken suggested at the 1985 Symposium. The situation may be somewhat analogous to what commentator Robert Chambers sees facing the World Bank. "Normal professionalism," he observes, has been reflected over the years in the Bank's traditional approach to development, measured by economic indicators and using predominantly western technologies. "In contrast, the new professionalism, already represented in the Bank, reverses the values, research methods, roles and power relations of normal professionalism, putting people first and poor people first of all." The new professionalism, he suggests, emphasizes decentralization, empowerment, local initiative, and diversity.[17]

In the case of humanitarian assistance, agencies which have proven themselves able to reach people in traditional settings of need are now being challenged to provide effective assistance in conflict situations where the best approaches are anything but self-evident. That a new degree of professionalism is required of aid providers is not a judgment on the lack of PVO professionalism in an earlier day and age. It is instead an acknowledgement of the greater complexity of today's conflicts and the greater role played by political factors in today's humanitarian crises.

Is Non-Political Humanitarian Assistance Possible?

Good intentions are not an appropriate foundation for good programs. Agencies' attempts to ignore the context of the Ethiopian famine by burying their heads in the sand and claiming political neutrality cannot be accepted. Finding out as much information as possible about a situation in which it is directly involved in an agency's only hope for remaining neutral. Sticking one's head in the sand is to take sides; it is a political act. . . .

[Each] relief and development agency operating in Ethiopia is political, each has its own agenda, albeit hidden, its own ideological leanings and its own assumptions about what constitutes appropriate relief and development activities. In short, agencies have no desire to remain neutral. . . .

Is it possible to give nonpolitical, humanitarian assistance? In an absolute sense, probably not. However, the best way to remain neutral in such situations is to keep informed.

Jason W. Clay, "The West and the Ethiopian Famine: Implications for Humanitarian Assistance," 1986.

If the InterAction discussions have not left a finished product of timeless stature, they have raised the level of interest among PVOs in establishing some principles and ground rules to guide individual organizations in their decision-making and operations. This would itself represent a step in the direction of greater professionalism. To assist in that ongoing effort, materials are provided in the Appendices, including some questions for practitioners (III), sample guidelines used in training the overseas staff of one PVO (IV), and bibliographic resources for further reference (V).

The InterAction community, however, is of far from a single mind as to what a new professionalism would involve. There is some talk among PVOs in the U.S. and abroad of establishing a code of conduct by which private agencies might, on their own initiative, encourage higher performance and greater accountability. The need for some clearer standards was noted at several points in the dialogue, particularly with respect to the emergence of new PVOs working in Central America.

If the InterAction process produced no clear consensus about how to enhance the professionalism of PVOs, it also demonstrated a certain reluctance among PVOs to consider major initiatives in that direction. While achieving more clarity on issues of humanitarian assistance policy was felt to be needed, neither PVOs nor the U.S. government appeared particularly seized with the task of doing so. Both were more comfortable with concentrating on providing humanitarian aid and leaving the policy debate for another day.

The PVO survey (Appendix II) found that most agencies providing humanitarian assistance had working understandings of such aid to guide them in facing troublesome policy or operational issues. Many, however, felt that they did not possess adequate resources to deal with basic humanitarian aid issues, suggesting a certain vulnerability at the very time they seek to distinguish themselves from practitioners of do-it-yourself humanitarianism newly appearing on the scene. The fact that, within InterAction, humanitarian assistance has had to vie for attention with higher priority issues further illustrates the problem.

On the government side, meanwhile, U.S. officials are much more comfortable engaging PVOs on operational than on policy matters. Instead of using their time with Deputy Secretary of State Whitehead to discuss the nature of humanitarian assistance and other major policy issues, PVOs were advised by State Department aides to focus on forging new collaborative arrangements so that "something practical" would come of the meeting. In the meeting itself, the denial of access for people to humanitarian assistance in Central America was treated as a relatively minor matter.

The difficulties experienced by the PVO community in dealing with humanitarian aid issues suggest that it may be unrealistic to seek community-wide agreement on a code of conduct or a statement of policy. If the draft InterAction Statement is any indication, the problems of achieving consensus correlate directly with the degree of specificity sought. The more general the views expressed, the more acceptable — but also the less meaningful. The Statement is helpful in committing PVOs, as "our awareness of the complexities of humanitarian assistance increases, to enhancing our own effectiveness and professionalism as providers of humanitarian aid." Taking an additional step, however, to exclude non-reputable PVOs from the community could prove a contentious and unproductive exercise.

Indeed, a more prescriptive approach might prove unwise as well as unrealistic. In objecting to the loose use of the term "humanitarian assistance" to characterize aid to the Contras, PVOs were cautioned against pressing the Administration or the Congress to formulate a definition which, while more precise, might from a PVO vantage point turn out to be unduly restrictive. It may prove more productive instead for PVOs to extend and deepen the discussion process so that individual agencies in their day-to-day activities may proceed with greater wisdom and effectiveness.

The need perceived by PVOs to enhance their professionalism has implications for InterAction as their professional association. InterAction has played a central role in the discussions to date in part because the complexity of the issues makes them difficult for any single agency to take on. That role has been valuable even though there are, in numerical terms, about as many American PVOs registered with AID which are not InterAction members as those which are.

InterAction is well-positioned to familiarize the PVO community with the efforts of individual PVOs to develop policy for themselves in this area. In the years since the InterAction dialogue began, agencies such as the Mennonite Central Committee, Oxfam America, Church World Service, and the National Council of Churches have formulated or updated their policies. World Vision South Africa has issued a statement committing itself to stepped up advocacy efforts with the South African government. Even though InterAction has approved no policy on Contra aid, some PVOs individually and together have expressed their views. InterAction could assure that such efforts enrich the PVO community as a whole.

At various points in the process, InterAction has been requested not only to plan additional discussions of humanitarian aid but to provide case studies of recent and emerging conflict situations for review by interested agencies. A Working Group on Southern Africa currently meets on a regular basis to discuss humanitarian aid and related issues. The Migration and Refugee Committee, as noted earlier, carries out a full agenda of discussions bearing directly on humanitarian aid. The Public Policy Committee may also return to the issue in the coming years.

Aid and Ideology

In a country strongly divided by political ideologies, unfortunately even those who bring humanitarian assistance sometimes channel their funding based on these ideologies. Despite many visits by AID officials and U.S. Ambassador Thomas Pickering, the [Catholic] archdiocese [of El Salvador] has been reluctant to participate in a U.S.-sponsored humanitarian assistance program for the country. The contention of the archdiocese is, "Why should we accept funding for humanitarian assistance from one hand when, from the other, the military accepts arms that have caused the problem in the first place? Both the military and the administration prefer a military victory rather than dialogue. We have no choice but to refuse."

Other private agencies have also decided not to work with AID in El Salvador. Among the agencies following the position of the archdiocese are: [Catholic Relief Services,] The Lutheran Church of El Salvador, the Mennonite Central Committee, Medecins du Monde, World Vision, and others. In several interviews . . . two reasons for this decision were cited: questions about security for personnel working on AID-sponsored projects; and concern about political identification with U.S. policy in El Salvador. . . . [On the other hand,] some organizations in El Salvador do participate [with AID, including] the Union of Salvadoran Evangelical Churches (CESAD), Project Hope, and ... the Knights of Malta. ... There is no central coordinating agency to assure the delivery of relief and development assistance.

U.S. Committee for Refugees,"Aiding the Desplazados of El Salvador: The Complexity of Humanitarian Assistance."

The need perceived by PVOs to enhance their professionalism also has implications for constituency education activities by PVOs in the United States. The meaning of impartiality, the ways in which PVOs come to terms more fully with political realities, and the tension between the two emerge from the InterAction process as the items most in need of further reflection within the PVO family and with the larger public.

In paradoxical fashion, then, the InterAction dialogue suggests the need for PVOs to become at one and the same time more scrupulously apolitical and more politically astute. American citizens, whose humanitarian concern PVOs seek to express, are also inhabitants of a complex and conflict-laden planet. In the final analysis, they are as ill-served by aid which purports to assist people in a political vacuum as by aid which makes humanitarianism a political crusade.

The politicization of humanitarian assistance undercuts the effectiveness of PVOs as aid providers, whether such aid be treated an extension of U.S. foreign policy or as a device for critiquing U.S. foreign policy. PVOs which make the test of their humanitarian assistance its compatibility with U.S. foreign policy may have difficulty explaining how such aid can follow the flag and still meet international expectations of impartiality. PVOs which maintain that their aid is humanitarian just because it goes where the American flag does not may be hard-pressed to explain their lack of responsiveness to the urgent needs of persons who happen to be located in countries of particular interest to the United States government.

Humanitarian assistance, the InterAction conversations suggest, does not validate or invalidate itself by virtue of its relation, positive or negative, to U.S. foreign policy. Humanitarian assistance does not become authentic simply by virtue of being called humanitarian, whether by the U.S. government or by U.S. private organizations. It distinguishes itself instead by its effective and accountable responsiveness to critical human needs, wherever people are suffering.

If the InterAction dialogue has highlighted the harmful effects of the politicization of humanitarian assistance, it has also suggested that such politicization is not inevitable. Adapting their well established and highly respected traditions of humanitarian assistance to the challenges of functioning in highly politicized settings, PVOs may acquit themselves well in the complex but urgent task of helping people in an age of conflict.

EPILOGUE

The urgency of continuing to struggle with the issues raised during the InterAction dialogue has been underscored by late-breaking events. In the course of a single week in late October 1987, for example, as this review was being prepared, the following items were reported:

- The ambush of a convoy of relief vehicles bound for Tigray by Ethiopian rebels, who alleged that the trucks contained weapons. One driver was killed, other aid personnel wounded. Lost were 450 tons of wheat, 23 donated vehicles, and valuable momentum in pre-positioning food to avoid a recurrence of the 1984-85 famine experience.[1] More recent reports indicate that the Eritrean People's Liberation Front has committed itself to "take all possible precautions" to attack only military and not relief vehicles,[2] although the problem appears to be continuing.[3]

- The assassination of the president of El Salvador's non-governmental human rights commission, apparently at the hands of death squads. His murder was expected to complicate reconciliation between the government and the rebels.[4] Throughout the week the press reported on issues related to the implementation of the regional peace agreement for Central America, including the role of external aid and the provisions for reconstruction and for resettlement of refugees and displaced persons.[5]

- The further deterioration of Lebanon's economy, with the International Monetary Fund projecting an inflation rate for 1987 as high as 400 percent. "About 1.2 million people, about a third of Lebanon's population, need help." Save the Children's food distribution director reports that because of the economic crisis, "families, especially children, [are] beginning to show signs of malnutrition." Members of warring militias are said to be selling their weapons to buy food.[6]

- The shelling from within Cambodia of an area in Thailand near Site 8, a camp housing about 31,000 Cambodian refugees. While the refugees were not evacuated, aid agencies personnel may soon be. "Cambodian guerrillas are fighting Vietnamese troops occupying Cambodia, with the war sometimes straying into Thailand and inflicting casualties on Thais and on Cambodian refugees in border camps aided by the United Nations. [The Site 8 camp] ... is controlled by the Khmer Rouge, the strongest of the three major guerrilla groups."[7]

• The devastating effects of the increasingly barbarous war between Iran and Iraq on their civilian populations, particularly children. A report by the Center on War and the Child estimates that at least 50,000 Iranian children have been killed in combat, some as participants in human wave attacks, others while serving as human minesweepers. Iraqi children have suffered from the war as well.[8]

• The confirmation of the deaths of two Americans filming a documentary in Afghanistan for CAUSA, a private organization founded in 1980 by the Rev. Sun Myung Moon. Newspapers also carried ads soliciting contributions to a U.S. PVO providing cross-border medical assistance from Pakistan following the reported systematic destruction of hospitals and clinics and the arrests of civilian medical personnel in resistance-held areas by Soviet forces.[9]

• The capture in Sri Lanka by Indian troops of the Tamil rebel stronghold of Jaffna, in the wake of the collapse of a peace agreement and the resumption of attacks on civilian and military targets by the Liberation Tigers of Tamil Eelam. As India stepped up its effort to provide humanitarian aid to Jaffna, "More and more, one hears comparisons with the permanent divisions and alien occupation forces of two other troubled islands, Ireland and Cyprus."[10]

• A shift in the U.S. sanctuary movement from transporting Central Americans to the U.S. to assisting those already here and generating pressure for changes in U.S. policy toward the region. U.S. government figures place the number of Salvadorans in the U.S. in the range of 500,000 — 800,000 and of Guatemalans at about 150,000.[11]

Such developments — and scarcely a week passes without them — reinforce the importance of committing ongoing attention to the issues of the principles and practice of humanitarian assistance raised during the InterAction dialogue. The needs to which PVOs are nowadays called to respond are indeed set amidst conflicts and enmeshed in complexities: national and international, political, ideological, economic, racial, ethnic, social, and religious.

Sustaining the dialogue on these issues, however, will not be easy. A number of considerations, some deeply rooted in the culture of the U.S. and of U.S. PVOs, may make enhanced professionalism as difficult as it is desirable.

First, there are continuing doubts that a humanitarian assistance policy is really necessary. Since PVOs exist to help people, why would they not provide aid whenever and wherever it is required? How would deferred action be explained to contributors who place a premium on meeting human need swiftly? The action orientation of PVOs will generally win out over the need also to reflect on situational complexities. The simpler professionalism of an earlier day has enduring appeal.

Second, even if such a policy is necessary, there are doubts that it is feasible. PVOs view their overseas personnel as seasoned and resourceful professionals, fully able to make on-the-spot judgments. Since aid activities are always country-specific, limited value is attached to formulating agency-wide policy and providing personnel training for future contingencies. Decisions are best left, the reasoning goes, to staff who are closer to the action.

Third, many PVOs welcome their partnership with governments and find in it no unmanageable constraints upon voluntary action. They would not accept U.S. government funds, they say, which compromised their integrity. They are more comfortable providing aid to people in areas for which the U.S. government makes assistance available than in areas where the U.S. government provides no assistance, or discourages others from providing it. After all, the purpose of PVOs is to provide aid, not to challenge the U.S. government.

PVOs also acknowledge that host governments establish the contexts in which they carry out their activities. They are quick to point out that they would not work in settings in which their missions were compromised. Again, however, such judgments are best made on the scene. There is little which policy formulation or handbook guidelines can do, many feel, to affect or predict the local contexts in which situational judgments will need to be reached.

Finally, even while PVOs acknowledge the need for a new level of professionalism, the pressures on operational agencies to respond to burgeoning human need may limit their ability to wrestle with their responsibilities and accountabilities as aid providers. Moreover, the circumscribed resources available to individual agencies may discourage individual PVOs from developing or retaining the requisite expertise in matters of international law. The heterogeneity of the PVO community as a whole may limit how much is done jointly in this area.

The InterAction dialogue, reinforced by ongoing events, has demonstrated the importance of developing greater professionalism among U.S. providers of voluntary humanitarian assistance, however difficult that process be. Continuing attention to issues of humanitarian policy and practice constitutes essential unfinished business for the U.S. PVO community in the years ahead.

The Ongoing Task

Implementation of the principles of the Geneva Conventions and Protocols is a constant struggle being waged everywhere: through the actions of individuals who press on governments their concern for the humane treatment of people, through agencies providing humanitarian assistance on the spot, and through concerted action by the international community.

Michel Veuthey, International Committee of the Red Cross, 1987.

ENDNOTES

Chapter I

[1]James N. Purcell Jr., "Humanitarian Assistance under Fire," (U.S. Department of State Public Information Series, 21 May 1986), p. 1.

[2]Except where otherwise indicated, citations from InterAction events are taken from organization records or the notes of participants.

[3]Alexandre Hay, "ICRC Appeal for Humanity," p. 5.

[4]Ibid., pp. 6-7.

[5]Independent Commission on International Humanitarian Issues, *Modern Wars: The Humanitarian Challenge* (Atlantic Highlands, NJ and London: Zed Books, Ltd., 1986), p. 24.

[6]Ibid., p. 25.

[7]Ibid.

[8]Ibid., p. 37.

[9]Cf. letter of 13 March 1986 from eight private agencies to Members of Congress, reprinted in the *Congressional Record* of 18 March 1986 (Vol. 132, No. 33), p. S2966.

[10]Christine E. Contee, "What Americans Think: Views on Development and U.S.-Third World Relations" (InterAction and the Overseas Development Council: New York and Washington, DC 1987), p. 15.

[11]Ibid., p. 28.

[12]Ibid., pp. 24-5.

[13]Ibid., p. 10.

[14]Ibid., p. 11.

[15]Ibid., p. 25.

[16]Ibid.

[17]Ibid., p. 51.

[18]Paul A. Laudicina, *World Poverty and Development: A Survey of American Opinion* (Washington, DC: Overseas Development Council, 1973), p. 106.

[19]Contee, *What Americans Think,* p. 27.

[20]Ibid., p. 14.

[21]InterAction, *Diversity in Development: U.S. Voluntary Assistance to Africa* (Washington, DC: InterAction, 1985)

[22]*Washington Post*, 3 January 1987, p. A1.

[23]*Washington Post*, 19 November 1987, p. A26.

[24]Military and Paramilitary Activities in and against Nicaragua (Nicaragua v. United States of America), Merits, Judgment, *International Court of Justice Reports,* 1986, p. 14, para. 243.

Chapter II

[1]Letter from Williams to McPherson, 29 July 1985.

[2]Father Jenco was released on 26 July 1986.

[3]Jean-Jacques Surbeck, "The Rights and Responsibilities of PVOs as Humanitarian Assistance Providers from the Perspective of International Law and Customs," pp. 6-9. Surbeck's description of the qualities of humanitarian assistance is based on the authoritative Commentaries to the Geneva Conventions by Jean Pictet. Additional material related to the ICRC is found on pages 7-8 and 40-1, in the feature boxes on pages 63 and 74, and in the bibliographical entry by Peter T. White on page 97.

[4]The United States is a party to the four Geneva Conventions of 1949 but has yet to ratify the two additional Protocols of 1977. The Reagan

Administration has asked the Senate to ratify Protocol II, which clarifies the protections due to victims in non-international conflicts. It has indicated that it does not intend to forward Protocol I for ratification, believing it undermines existing humanitarian law by granting wars of national liberation international status, protecting victims of such conflicts accordingly. Treaties become the law of the land upon ratification. The Protocols are also mentioned in the discussion of the ICRC on pp. 7-8 and in the feature box on page 63.

[5] Joseph A. Mitchell, "U.S. Law and Regulations as Regards 'Humanitarian Assistance': The Impact on American Voluntary Agencies," p. 5.

[6] Ibid., p. 9.

[7] Kemper's views are elaborated in *Sojourners* Magazine, October 1985: "Contras, Refugees, and Private Aid: Who Benefits, Who Suffers?" The activities of private groups are also detailed in the *Miami Herald* 21 January 1985, the *Washington Post* 3 May 1985, and in *The New Right Humanitarians* (Inter-Hemispheric Education Resource Center, Albuquerque, NM, 1986).

[8] The U.S. Congress provided $7.5 million in 1984 for Miskito and other Nicaraguan Indians with the stipulation that it be administered by AID "independently from United Nations relief agencies [and] solely for humanitarian purposes." (House Appropriations Report, Second Supplemental Appropriations Bill, 1984, pp. 88-9.) The feature box on p. 53 (item 6) also addresses this issue, as does the entry by Juliana Geron Pilon on page 100.

[9] Purcell, "Humanitarian Assistance Under Fire," p. 2.

[10] Ibid., p. 3.

[11] Ibid.

[12] Ibid.

[13] Details of the license applications for shipments to Nicaragua are provided in Oxfam America, "Contradictions and Inconsistencies in Humanitarian Assistance to the Contras," (Boston: 1986). The details of its requests for Vietnam and Kampuchea are provided in Joel R. Charney and John Spragens, Jr., *Obstacles to Recovery in Vietnam and Kampuchea: U.S. Embargo of Humanitarian Aid* (Boston: Oxfam America, 1984),

pp. 140-3.

[14]This issue has been the subject of considerable subsequent discussion within and among PVOs.

[15]Michael Sinclair, *Community Development in South Africa: A Guide for American Donors* (Washington, DC: Investor Responsibility Research Center, Inc., 1986) pp. 1, 18.

Chapter III

[1]The most recent data on PVOs is available in AID's "Voluntary Foreign Aid Programs 1986" (Washington, DC: 1987). Information about InterAction member agencies is available in *Member Profiles* and *Addendum* (New York: InterAction, 1987).

[2]Pierre Bergeron, *The Rights of the Oppressed in Humanitarian Law* (New York: Church World Service, 1983.)

[3]Independent Commission, *Modern Wars*, pp. 32-3.

[4]Joel R. Charny and Joseph Short, "Voluntary Aid Inside Kampuchea," in Barry S. Levy and Daniel C. Susott, eds., *Years of Horror, Days of Hope: Responding to the Cambodian Refugee Crisis* (Millwood, NY, New York City, and London: Associated Faculty Press, 1987), p. 262.

[5]Independent Commission, *Modern Wars*, p. 37.

[6]Bruce Nichols, "Rubberband Humanitarianism," in *Ethics and International Affairs*, Volume 1, 1987, pp. 206-7.

[7]U.S. AID, *Displaced Persons in El Salvador: An Assessment* (Washington, DC: 1984), pp. 16-7.

[8]Michael Sinclair, *Community Development in South Africa*, p. 68.

[9]Private conversation with Larry Minear.

[10]InterAction, 1988 Operation Plan and Budget, approved by the Board of Directors, 10 November 1987.

[11]Letter dated 16 October 1986 from Robert E. Gribben, Deputy Director, Office of East African Affairs, U.S. Department of State, to the Mennonite Central Committee, p. 1.

[12]Current AID policy is elaborated in "A.I.D. Partnership in International Development with Private and Voluntary Organizations," (Washington, DC: 1982).

[13]Cornelio Sommaruga, "The Protocols Additional to the Geneva Conventions: A Quest for Universality," *International Review of the Red Cross*, No. 258 (May—June 1987), p. 246.

[14]Quoted in Independent Commission, *Modern Wars*, p. 47.

[15]Stephen Dujack, American Foreign Service Association, conversation with the author, 24 November 1987.

[16]Alexandre Hay, in *Modern Wars*, p. 47.

[17]Robert Chambers, "Poverty, Environment and the World Bank: The Opportunity for a New Professionalism," September 1987 (unpublished), p. 4.

Epilogue

[1]*Washington Post*, 26 October 1987.

[2]*Washington Post*, 1 December 1987.

[3]*Christian Science Monitor*, 22 January 1988.

[4]*New York Times*, 28 October 1987.

[5]Cf., for example, *New York Times*, 22 and 24 October 1987.

[6]*Washington Post*, 26 October 1987.

[7]Associated Press, 27 October 1987.

[8]*Christian Science Monitor*, 28 October 1987.

[9]*Washington Post*, 29 October 1987

[10]*New York Times*, 28 October 1987.

[11]*New York Times*, 27 October, 1987.

Feature Boxes

Page 9: "Humanitarian Law at A Time of Failing National and International Consensus: A Report for the Independent Commission on International Humanitarian Issues," in *Modern War: The Humanitarian Challenge* (Atlantic Highlands, NJ and London: Zed Books, Ltd., 1986), p. 26.

Page 14: *Time*, 21 December 1987, p. 37.

Page 18: Robert A. Seiple, President, World Vision United States, in *World Vision* Magazine, Vol. 31, No. 6 (December 1987—January 1988), p. 3.

Page 22: Military and Paramilitary Activities in and against Nicaragua (Nicaragua v. United States of America), Merits, Judgment, *International Court of Justice Reports*, 1986, p. 14, para. 242.

Page 25: Joel R. Charny and Joseph Short, "Voluntary Aid Inside Kampuchea," in Barry S. Levy and Daniel C. Susott, eds., *Years of Horror, Days of Hope: Responding to the Cambodian Refugee Crisis* (Millwood, NY, New York City, and London: Associated Faculty Press, 1987), pp. 260-1. The entry by William Shawcross on p. 101 also deals with this subject.

Page 30: "Food for the Hungry without Regard to Politics: An Interview with M. Peter McPherson, Administrator, Agency for International Development," *U.S. News & World Report*, 13 May 1985, p. 37.

Page 34: Charles Villa-Vicencio, "Interview," in *Southern Africa Development News*, Vol. 2, No. 1 (January 1988), p. 11 (a publication of Inter-Action).

Page 36: *Washington Times* Editorial, "Resistance Aid, not Party Games," 10 May 1985, p. 9A.

Page 40: Corinne Johnson, American Friends Service Committee Bulletin, No. 157, Vol. 68, No. 2 (Spring 1987), p. 2.

Page 41: Independent Commission, *Modern Wars*, pp. 28-9.

Page 48: Letter of 16 October 1986 from Robert E. Gribben, Deputy Director, Office of East African Affairs, U.S. Department of State, to the the Mennonite Central Committee, p. 1.

Page 53: AID, *Displaced Persons in El Salvador: An Assessment* (Washington, DC: 1984), pp. 16-7.

Page 59: U.S. Coordinator for Refugee Affairs Jonathan Moore, addressing the Executive Committee of the U.N. High Commissioner for Refugees, 6 October 1987.

Page 63: Alexandre Hay, in the Independent Commission, *Modern Wars*, pp. 49-50.

Page 66: Jason W. Clay, "The West and the Ethiopian Famine: Implications for Humanitarian Assistance," (Cambridge, MA: Cultural Survival, 1986), pp. 17-8 and 47.

Page 69: U.S. Committee for Refugees, "Aiding the Desplazados of El Salvador: The Complexity of Humanitarian Assistance," (Washington, DC: U.S. Committee for Refugees), 1984, pp. 16-7.

Page 74: Michel Veuthey, Head of the International Organizations Division, International Committee of the Red Cross, interview with the author, 2 October 1987.

APPENDIX I
DRAFT INTERACTION STATEMENT
ON HUMANITARIAN ASSISTANCE

This Statement, which was drafted by the Working Group on Humanitarian Assistance, was circulated among InterAction members beginning in 1985. It was refined to reflect insights from the various events in the InterAction dialogue. Twenty-three member agencies have endorsed it as their own policy and InterAction's, three have expressed reservations. Since unanimity is required to establish InterAction policy, this text does not have that status.

This is a statement of InterAction policy on the nature of humanitarian assistance and the safeguards needed to protect its integrity. InterAction is a participatory association of U.S. private and voluntary organizations (PVOs) engaged in providing humanitarian assistance as an integral part of a larger commitment to helping the world's people achieve greater self-reliance, justice, and peace.

1. Humanitarian assistance, in which PVOs have been actively involved for generations, is assistance provided in response to urgent and unmet basic human needs. It encompasses such items as food, medicines and medical supplies, shelter, clothing, water and basic household supplies delivered in a way that sustains people in need and enhances their potential to become self-reliant.

2. Our definition of humanitarian assistance draws heavily on international custom and tradition. The Geneva Conventions, which are central to the established international understanding of humanitarian assistance, provide ground rules to guide the major providers of such assistance -- PVOs, governments, and international organizations -- in conflict situations. Humanitarian assistance must be offered impartially (i.e., independently from parties to a conflict) and strictly on the basis of need, free from extraneous objectives and managed by entities which can assure its efficacy. The right to humanitarian assistance is recognized in the Geneva Conventions only for civilians (and prisoners of war) and not for combatants.

3. We welcome the Geneva Convention's recognition of the right of PVOs to offer to provide humanitarian assistance and their encouragement to governments to allow humanitarian assistance activities to be carried out without interference. PVOs which choose to operate in conflict situations need to do so with a sensitivity to the complexities involved. To the extent that PVOs accept resources from governments and international agencies, we need to assure ourselves that such resources neither compromise our delivery of humanitarian assistance as defined above nor undermine our impartiality. We

believe that only those organizations which adhere to the above principles should qualify as humanitarian.

4. As our awareness of the complexities of humanitarian assistance increases, we commit ourselves to enhancing our own effectiveness and professionalism as providers of humanitarian assistance.

APPENDIX II
INTERACTION QUESTIONNAIRE
ON HUMANITARIAN ASSISTANCE

This questionnaire was mailed to InterAction members in the fall of 1985. The responses of the twenty agencies which replied are tabulated here, along with selected comments.

1. Does your agency provide humanitarian assistance?

Yes 16   No 4

2. Does your agency have a working definition of "humanitarian assistance"?

Yes 12   No 7

Selected comments:
- We assume you are talking about "relief aid."
- We understand humanitarian assistance to mean material which meets human need.
- Our commitment is to provide quality water for those in need of it.
- We define "humanitarian assistance" as that which gives low-income women skills to become self-sufficient economically in order to be able to improve the quality of life for themselves and their families.

3. Have questions about the nature of humanitarian assistance (e.g., whether it could be made available with integrity in a given situation) figured in any recent programming decisions of your agency?

Yes 15   No 5

Sample answers:
- No, as a PVO what we do is not with any political connection. However we do coordinate information with the host government.
- Yes, we carefully assess whether it is possible to help women within the social and political framework of any developing country. We also believe it very important for us as a PVO to be perceived as apolitical in any country in which we work. Increasing support for the full participation of women in economic development in many countries of the world is sensitive work.

4. Check those agencies with which you have worked during the past several years:

    17 USAID
    10 U.S. Department of State
    10 U.N. High Commissioner for Refugees (UNHCR)

5 U.N. Disaster Relief Organization (UNDRO)
5 International Committee of the Red Cross (ICRC)
15 Individual developing country governments
20 "Indigenous" private voluntary organizations
5 Other [responses include other U.S. and international PVOs, the U.S. Information Agency, other U.N. agencies, the aid agencies of other governments, and local communities]

5. **Have you sensed a growing public concern about the politicization of humanitarian aid?**

        Yes 14   **No** 6

The Yes answers include "but not on a sustained basis," "in regard to Nicaragua," and "but not significantly enough."

The No answers include "only as it relates to relief assistance" and an appreciation for "whenever our government becomes involved in humanitarian aid through USAID or the State Department."

6. **Do questions related to the nature of humanitarian assistance figure occasionally in staff discussions?**

        Yes 17   **No** 3

7. **[If so,] do you have adequate resources at your disposal to answer them?**

        Yes 9   **No** 7

- We make phone calls to other organizations, our field offices, government contacts, missionaries or Peace Corps people familiar with the situation/region.
- We have a vast network of contacts.

8. **Are there specific countries or regions which you would like to see given special attention [in upcoming InterAction discussions]?**

- Central America (Nicaragua and El Salvador), the Caribbean and Latin America (Mexico, Peru)
- The Middle East
- Africa (Southern Africa, including Mozambique and the Transkei, the Horn of Africa, the Western Sudan, and Ethiopia, including Eritrea)
- Asia (including Afghanistan, Iran, Indochina, Thailand/Kampuchea, Bangladesh, Indonesia/East Timor, Korea, and the Philippines)
- The U.S.S.R.
- The Pacific Atoll Islands

9. Are there specific issues you would like to see addressed . . .?

- How humanitarian assistance is defined (4 respondents).
- The moral and religious basis of humanitarian concerns.
- The politics of starvation.
- How does a PVO help the refugees (women, children, etc.) without appearing to be political.
- Restrictions on the export of humanitarian goods to so-called enemy nations such as Vietnam and Cambodia.
- How to increase the capacity of indigenous NGOs.
- How U.S. government funds can have a deleterious effect on the independence of the private sector in developing countries.
- The possibility that PVOs should manage the U.S. bilateral programs in Africa so as to implement them more cost-effectively.
- How to keep long term development proceeding despite political unrest.
- Can humanitarian assistance successfully be phased into developmental assistance so as to prevent future famines (2 respondents).
- The role of international relief in incentives for work.
- The impact of trade, financial transactions, and private investment on the satisfaction of humanitarian needs.
- How to combat the myth that one hundred percent of donor dollars will go to the disaster area.

10. Is there someone on your staff whom you would like to have involved in the work of the . . . planning committee?
[Individual suggestions made]

11. Would you or another senior level official or board member be in a position to attend [upcoming events]?
[Substantial interest expressed]

APPENDIX III
SOME QUESTIONS FOR PRACTITIONERS

One of the recurring recommendations of the InterAction dialogue was that InterAction develop a set of guidelines to assist PVOs in their humanitarian aid activities. It was understood that the heterogeneity of the PVO community would require each ageny to formulate its own policies and procedures to guide its involvement in conflict situations. However, while agencies might reach different conclusions about whether or how to assist in a particular situation, each faces common issues and requires certain basic information.

For example, understanding the nature of a conflict and the host government's attitude toward it, the dialogue suggests, might have a bearing on the nature and terms of a PVO's involvement. One PVO might read the conflict and the government's approach to it differently from another, leading one to become involved and another to refrain. One agency might place a higher premium on responding to particular human need, another to avoiding the political entanglement such a response might involve. PVOs might assess the risks to the physical security of aid workers differently, affecting their respective decisions to deploy or recall staff. However divergent the answers, the issues which need to be addressed in each instance are common ones.

What follows, therefore, are generic questions to aid PVOs as they seek to come to grips with these issues, not model PVO policies and procedures ready for insertion into PVO manuals. The questions were compiled in 1986 on the basis of the InterAction dialogue, supplemented by interviews with members agencies. They have since been refined and will benefit from further adaption based on their use.

I. Assessment of Human Need and Available Resources

A basic element in deciding whether to provide humanitarian assistance, of what sorts, and in what amounts is an assessment of human need and of the resources likely to become available. Questions such as the following may be helpful in the assessment process.

A. *With respect to need,*

1. What is the nature of the need? To what extent are the needs of an emergency nature (e.g., food, medicine, clothing, shelter)? To what extent are they of a longer term developmental nature (e.g., food production, health training, technology transfer)?

2. What is the scale of human need in the country? Where is it located

geographically? What is its demography (e.g., by age, sex, racial or ethnic group, land tenure status)?

3. What are the best available assessments of current or recent need?

What is the extent of need according to the host government?

Are U.N. organization assessments available (e.g., the High Commissioner for Refugees, the Disaster Relief Organization, the Food and Agriculture Organization, the World Food Program, UNICEF)?

Have individual government agencies carried out recent assessments (e.g., AID or the Candian International Development Agency)?

Have private organizations (e.g., other PVOs, Amnesty International, or other human rights groups)?

4. To what extent are the assessments of need confirmed by evidence from local communities (e.g., the severity of food shortages by higher market prices or by more hoarding by households)?

5. What are the logistics of reaching people in need? Does the government have the infrastructure to do so? If not, how expensive and time-consuming will it be to develop one?

6. How do the needs of people in the conflict situation compare with those of the general population? Is it likely that attention to the former will create problems with the latter?

B. *With respect to resources,*

1. What resources are likely to be made available by the host government? Is it treating the situation as a major emergency? Is it, or will it soon be, actively seeking outside help?

2. What private humanitarian organizations, indigenous or expatriate, are active in the country? Do they function cooperatively, or are there areas of competition and tension? Is there a workable division of labor among them, geographically and/or functionally?

II. Assessment of Political Factors

The human needs to which PVOs seek to respond in non-political fashion are invariably set in a political context. The difficulties of providing human needs aid in stable situations are exacerbated when conflict is present. The following questions may therefore help PVOs develop an awareness of the political

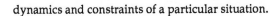

dynamics and constraints of a particular situation.

A. *The Nature of the Unrest*

1. What is the level of civil unrest? Is it intense enough to warrant the label "conflict"?

2. What are the underlying reasons for the unrest? How deep-seated and pervasive does it seem to be? How long-lived has it proved? Is it likely to worsen? If so, how quickly?

3. To what extent is the unrest a hopeful sign of emerging changes in an unjust situation?

B. *Host Government Attitudes*

1. What is the general tenor of the government's response to the conflict? To what extent, if any, are development programs or other human needs activities carried out by the government affected by the situation?

2. How sensitive is the government about the conflict? Is it a national or international embarrassment? Is it viewed as a threat to its authority? Is the government's assessment of the extent of need likely to be accurate, or is it perhaps under- or over-estimated for political reasons?

3. What are the government's attitudes toward the people in need? Are there factors of an ethnic, tribal, religious, or political nature which may affect its willingness to assist?

4. How supportive is the government likely to be of efforts to involve the affected people themselves in assistance programs? Are there patterns of human rights violations which would affect the viability of efforts to involve the people themselves in the planning and execution of such programs?

5. What is the state of relations between the host government and the U.S. government? Is the relationship likely to have a major bearing on the activities undertaken by a U.S. PVO?

6. Are there political parties, factions, or other forces within the country whose views of the conflict or of outside assistance are likely to affect the functioning of outside agencies?

C. *Humanitarian Assistance*

1. How receptive is the government to outside assistance? Has it requested such aid? Are efforts to assist likely to be perceived as an assault on its sovereignty or a criticism of its effectiveness? Will the government provide

the necessary access to people in need? What is the tenor of current relationships between the government and existing aid providers, whether multilateral, bilateral, or private?

2. Is the government a party to the Geneva Conventions and Protocols? How would it respond to questions regarding its compliance? What has been its record historically in observing international law and custom? How sensitive is it to international public opinion?

3. How viable is the private sector? Do indigenous PVOs exist? What kind of relations do they enjoy with the government? How do they view the involvement of expatriate PVOs in providing humanitarian aid? What are their views about partnership arrangements? Would they utilize U.S. government as well as privately generated American resources?

4. What is the general state of PVO/government relations? Are expatriate PVOs a known commodity? Does the government have a coordinating mechanism for dealing with them? Is it likely to be responsive to, or resistant to, dealing with PVOs as a community?

5. Is the government business-like in its dealings with PVOs? Is it likely to sign the necessary agreements with expatriate PVOs and to abide by them? Does a PVO which conducts itself professionally stand a good chance of having its agreements extended by a subsequent government?

6. What effects is the proposed humanitarian assistance likely to have on power relations within the society? Are those effects likely over the longer term to enhance the prospects of the poor?

III. Decision-Making

A review of the needs and their political context supplies PVOs with some key elements for deciding whether to provide humanitarian assistance. Arriving at a decision may be facilitated by questions such as the following:

A. *Geneva Conventions and Protocols*

1. Will the PVO be able to function as a humanitarian agency, that is, to respond to human beings as such, unaffected by political or military considerations?

From the PVO side, are its purposes and the resources it provides free from extraneous agendas?

From the host government side, will a PVO be granted adequate freedom of operation and access to those in need?

2. Will the PVO be able to function impartially, that is, to provide relief solely on the basis of need without distinctions imposed by the host or other governments or from other quarters?

3. Will the PVO be able to meet the Geneva Convention expectations of efficacy: that is, will it have the necessary financial, material and staff resources and expertise to carry out the activities it undertakes?

4. If the PVO believes that aid should be provided irrespective of the relation of recipients to the conflict, will its involvement contribute to the equitable division of available human resources among the various sides?

B. *The Nature of the Assistance*

1. What distinctive contribution (in relation to assistance made available from other private and governmental agencies) would the PVO provide? Is it such as to justify in-country presence? How will its assistance be related to that of other international non-governmental aid providers? To indigenous institutions?

2. For what period would a PVO commit itself to provide aid? Is the time-frame long enough to have an impact on the situation and short enough to avoid becoming a permanent part of the picture? Does the government or the PVO assume that humanitarian aid will be followed up by reconstruction and development activities?

3. Are the physical risks to staff and program ones that the PVO is prepared to assume? What plans would it make for emergency evacuation of staff, if need be, and for continuation of program, if possible? What arrangements would be made for the routine rotation of staff to ease the duress involved?

4. Does the PVO have access to the resources (material or financial, technical or personnel) with which it can make a significant contribution? If the PVO were to use U.S. government resources, would these enhance or impair humanitarian aid activities? Would the U.S. government provide adequate flexibility and longevity in their use?

5. Would the PVO be able to provide adequate accountability to its board and, if U.S. government funds are involved, to the U.S. government? Would the costs of assuring such accountability be proportionate to the program involved? Could it be carried out with a minimum of intrusiveness?

C. *Other Considerations*

1. How does the provision of humanitarian assistance in this particular situation relate to the overall program and objectives of the PVO? If a PVO seeks to have activities in countries with a range of governmental or political sys-

tems, will assisting in this country help achieve that objective?

2. What are the impacts of becoming operationally involved likely to be on the PVO's work elsewhere in the country or region? What is the reaction of the U.S. government likely to be to its involvement, and how important is that reaction to the PVO in its decision-making?

3. If a PVO is committed to address the underlying causes of the conflict, will it be able to do so without compromising its ability to function in the country? For example, will it be able to press for a cease-fire at the same time that it treats war casualties? Are advocacy and education efforts in the United States likely jeopardize its in-country presence?

4. Does the PVO have the requisite expertise to interpret the complexities of the situation to its constituency and to respond to criticisms which may arise? If it decides to become involved, how would it respond to the charge that it is being used by the host government or prolonging the underlying problem? If it decides against involvement, how would it reply to those who might feel that humanitarian activities should have been undertaken?

IV. Reassessment

In conflict situations, which sometimes change rapidly, continued monitoring of developments and periodic reassessment of a PVO's involvement is needed.

1. What changes have occurred in the human needs situation? Is the situation improving? Is there continued need for PVO assistance? for a different kind or mix of aid? for a phase-down of activities?

2. Is the PVO being effective in meeting human need? What are the major constraints faced? If there are serious problems, how should they be addressed? What are the host (and U.S.) government views of progress to date?

3. Is the PVO meeting its responsibilities under the Geneva Conventions to respond to human need unimpeded by extraneous considerations?

4 Have the governments involved met their responsibilities? Is the PVO being given adequate access to people in need by the host government? Has the U.S. government, to the extent that it is involved, played a supportive role?

5. To what extent have the PVO's objectives been accomplished? If an objective was to strengthen local or national structures, has this been achieved? Are indigenous agencies now in a position to continue the program on their own?

6. Is the security of agency personnel in the country sufficient to justify the program's continuation? Are improved or alternative arrangements possible? How are staff bearing up under the stress associated with working and living amidst conflict?

7. Is progress being made to resolve the conflict? Are there ways in which the PVO could, if it deems such a role appropriate, help facilitate such a resolution?

8. What have been the effects, if any, of the program to date on power relations within the society?

9. How have the activities to date been received among constituents in the United States? Has adequate interpretation been provided so that contributors understand the complexities of the situation? Can continued support be counted on?

10. To what extent has the PVO, if this was its intention, brought the situation to the attention of the U.S. government? Is there additional advocacy which might be undertaken?

APPENDIX IV
SAMPLE GUIDELINES FOR AID
PERSONNEL IN CONFLICT SITUATIONS

In 1985 the Mennonite Central Committee(MCC) adopted guidelines for its personnel working in contested areas. Drawn from MCC experience since its founding in 1920, these learnings have subsequently become part of the regular training provided overseas volunteer staff. Upwards of five hundred MCC volunteers are engaged in international relief and development activities each year, a substantial number of them in conflict situations.

1. The Mennonite Central Committee (MCC) is committed to responding to human need "regardless of race, creed or political persuasion, realizing that such faithfulness may lead to suffering."

2. MCC has considerable experience in working in a variety of contested areas, each having its own unique configuration of political, economic, military, ethnic and religious factors.

3. Working in contested areas is difficult, complex, risky and sometimes costly.

4. The compassionate, healing, reconciling presence of Christ is needed in contested areas, and becomes visible through caring persons.

5. Workers in contested areas need: a) a deep sense of Christian call and commitment, b) cultural sensitivity, c) emotional maturity, and d) political awareness.

6. A strong, basic Christian support group for every worker in contested areas is important.

7. The image of the church becomes distorted when the church fails to identify with the poor and the oppressed and its leaders support economic, political and military policies of a particular class or nation, placing loyalty to these above loyalty to God. Establishing a clear church identity as free as possible from national political and ideological identity is imperative if the church is to remain true to its universal nature and calling.

8. Personnel in contested areas provide a unique resource for interpreting and informing Mennonites, the larger church, the public and the governments of conditions in contested areas.

9. Relief and development aid distribution patterns reflect power and should be recognized as having political implications.

10. The presence of MCC workers in contested areas indicates some sharing of the risks of the people. Sometimes this has been a positive morale factor for the local communities and in some instances has served to lower the level of violence. MCC presence may also bring special risks to nationals who associate with foreign personnel.

11. There are situations where, for reasons of political chaos or highly unpredictable and untargeted violence, it has been wise for MCC workers to leave an area, at least temporarily.

12. Maintaining communication with all segments of the population in the contested area to the degree possible and quietly interpreting MCC purposes, including the search for nonviolent alternatives, are important.

13. Governments and resistance movements have their own self-interests and motives and often attempt to utilize relief agencies for these purposes. MCC workers risk being suspected or charged with working for the CIA or for other special groups.

14. Service representatives from North American agencies are not always welcome in contested areas. They may be greeted with degrees of suspicion and hatred because of the link between Western military, economic and political policies and the conditions of oppression and poverty in the contested areas. Close identification with local people and customs in a posture of service is often the most significant witness in such situations. Effective workers seek to establish an identity that clearly reflects membership in Christ's new community which embodies peace and justice for all peoples.

15. Working on both sides of a conflict is one way to reflect the universal character of the church and its concern for all who suffer and are in need.

APPENDIX V
RESOURCES FOR FURTHER REFERENCE

In the interest of encouraging ongoing reflection on humanitarian assistance issues, a list of resource materials is provided, with brief comments on individual entries as appropriate. Modelled on bibliographies which provided background for discussions at the 1985 Symposium and the 1986 Forum, the list has been updated to include items which have since become available and materials currently in preparation. A number of the sixty-plus entries have been produced by, or suggested by, PVOs.

The list reflects a high degree of selectivity. (A recent bibliography published by the International Committee of the Red Cross on international law in conflict situations contains 6,640 entries.) The guiding considerations have been timeliness, utility, and accessibility to U.S. PVOs. Regional references emphasize the areas studied most closely during the InterAction dialogue. Addresses of institutions with regular publications and mailing lists have been provided.

I. General Works on PVOs

Interaction. *Member Profiles* and *Addendum*. New York: InterAction, 1987.

Drabek, Anne G., ed. "Development Alternatives: The Challenge for Non-Governmental Organizations." *World Development* 15 (Fall 1987 Supplement).

Egeland, Jan, ed. "Humanitarian Organization-Building in the Third World." *Bulletin of Peace Proposals* 18 No. 2 (1987).

Gorman, Robert, ed. *Private Voluntary Organizations as Agents of Development*. Boulder, CO and London: Westview Press, 1984.

Lissner, Jorgen. *The Politics of Altruism: A Study of the Political Behaviour of Voluntary Development Agencies*. Geneva, Switzerland: Lutheran World Federation, 1977.

Nichols, Bruce. "Rubberband Humanitarianism." *Ethics & International Affairs*, 1 (1987).

Schmidt, Elizabeth; Blewett, Jane; and Henriot, Peter. *Religious PVOs and the Question of Government Funding*. Maryknoll, NY: Orbis Books, 1981.

U.S. Agency for International Development. "A.I.D. Partnership in International Development with Private and Voluntary Organizations." Washington, DC: 1982.

———. "Voluntary Foreign Aid Programs 1986." Washington, DC: 1987.

White, Peter T. "A Little Humanity Amid the Horrors of War." *National Geographic* 170, No. 5 (November 1986). A pictorial essay on the International Committee of the Red Cross as "the conscience of an imperfect world."

II. International Humanitarian Law and Institutions

Macalister-Smith, Peter. *International Humanitarian Assistance: Disaster Relief Actions in International Law and Organization.* Boston: Martinus Nijhoff, 1985.

Bergeron, Pierre. *The Rights of the Oppressed in Humanitarian Law.* New York: Church World Service, 1983.

Egeland, Jan; Sandoz, Yves; and Doswald-Beck, Louise. "Special Issue on Humanitarian Law of Armed Conflict." *Bulletin of Peace Research,* 24 No. 3 (1987).

Forsythe, David P. *Humanitarian Politics.* Baltimore: Johns Hopkins University Press, 1977.

III. The Current Global Scene

Contee, Christine E. "What Americans Think: Views on Development and U.S.-Third World Relations." (A Public Opinion Project of InterAction and the Overseas Development Council) New York and Washington: 1987.

Cornia, Giovanni A.; Jolly, Richard; and Stewart, Frances. *Adjustment with a Human Face: Protecting the Vulnerable and Promoting Growth.* Oxford: Clarendon Press, 1987. (A United Nations Children's Fund publication)

The Heritage Foundation, a public policy research institute which seeks to articulate the voices of responsible conservatism, publishes books, monographs, and studies on issues such as U.S. foreign policy, U.S. regional interests, and the United Nations. (214 Mass. Ave. N.E., Washington, D.C. 20002)

Independent Commission on International Humanitarian Issues. *Modern War: The Humanitarian Challenge.* Atlantic Highlands, NJ and London: Zed Books, Ltd., 1986. The address of the Commission is P.O. Box 83, 1211 Geneva 20 CIC, Switzerland.

International Committee for the Red Cross publishes an *Annual Report,* a bimonthly *Review,* and a monthly newsletter, *Dissemination,* which are available from the ICRC, 780 Third Avenue, Room 2802, New York, N.Y. 10017.

Kirkpatrick, Jeane J. "The Reagan Doctrine and U.S. Foreign Policy." Washington, D.C.: Heritage Foundation, 1985.

Lappe, Frances Moore; Schurman, Rachel; and Danaher, Kevin. *Betraying the National Interest*. San Francisco: Institute for Food and Development Policy, 1988.

Mellor, John W., and Gavian, Sarah. "Famine: Causes, Prevention, and Relief." Science 235 (Jan. 1987): 539-45.

Middle East Report [MERIP]. "The Struggle for Food." 16 No. 2 (March-April, 1987). Contains articles on the politics of famine relief in the Horn of Africa and on the struggle for food in Egypt and the Middle East.

The Overseas Development Council is a private organization engaged in research and education on the economic and social problems of developing countries as they affect the U.S. ODC publishes a series of pamphlets and books, including *U.S. Foreign Policy and the Third World: Agenda 1985-6*. (1717 Mass. Ave. N.W., Washington, DC 20036)

Shulman, Marshall D. , ed. *East-West Tensions in the Third World*. New York: W.W. Norton, 1986.

The U.S. Department of State publishes "Current Policies" and "Gist," available from PA/OAP, Bureau of Public Affairs, Room 5815A, U.S. Department of State, Washington, DC 20520. The Department's annual human rights report is available from the Superintendent of Documents, U.S. Government Printing Office, Washington, D.C. 20402.

The U.S. AID Office of Foreign Disaster Assistance (OFDA) publishes an annual report, available from OFDA, U.S. Department of State, Room 1262A New State, Washington, D.C. 20520. Disaster Situation Reports are available through the computer networking service CARINET. AID's annual report to the Congress on Child Survival is available from the Office of Health in the Science and Technology Bureau.

The Worldwatch Institute, a private research organization on global trends in the availability and management of resources, publishes annually the *State of the World* and, periodically, Worldwatch Papers and other books and pamphlets. (1776 Mass. Ave. N.W., Washington, DC 20036. Annual subscriptions $25)

IV. Refugee Needs, Policies, and Programs

Independent Commission on International Humanitarian Issues. *The Dynamics of Displacement*. Atlantic Highlands, NJ and London: Zed Books Ltd., 1987.

Loescher, Gilbert, and Scanlon, John. *Calculated Kindness: Refugees and America's Half-Open Door. 1945-Present.* New York: Free Press, 1986.

Loescher, Gilbert, ed. *Refugees: The International Regime.* Oxford: Oxford University Press, forthcoming.

Nichols, Bruce. *The Uneasy Alliance: Religion, Refugees, and U.S. Foreign Policy.* Oxford: Oxford University Press, forthcoming.

Refuge magazine, which covers international refugee issues, is published five times a year by the Refugee Documentation Project of York University (4700 Keele Street, Downsview, ONT N3J 2R6, Canada).

The Refugee Policy Group serves as an independent center of policy analysis and research on refugee issues. A list of publications is available from 1424 16th St. N.W. Suite 401, Washington, D.C. 20036.

The Refugee Studies Programme at Oxford University publishes numerous reports, papers, and books. A bibliography and individual titles are available from the Programme at Queen Elizabeth House, Oxford University, 21 St. Giles, Oxford OX1 3LA, England.

The United Nations High Commissioner for Refugees (UNHCR) publishes *Refugees,* a monthly available on request, and *Refugee Abstracts,* a quarterly available at $20 per year. The latter includes UNHCR Executive Committee actions and reviews of recent literature on refugee issues. (1718 Connecticut Avenue, N.W., Suite 200, Washington, D.C. 20036)

The U.S. Committee for Refugees is a private agency providing public information on refugee protection and assistance, particularly involving developing emergencies and little known-situations. Examples of publications in its Issue Papers and Issue Brief series are listed in the sections on Sub-Saharan Africa and Central America. (815 15th St. N.W., Suite 610, Washington, D.C. 20005)

V. Sub-Saharan Africa

Clay, Jason W., and Holcomb, Bonnie K. "Politics and the Ethiopian Famine, 1984-1985." Cambridge, MA: Cultural Survival, 1986.

Independent Commission on International Humanitarian Issues. *Famine: A Man-Made Disaster?* New York: Random House, 1985.

InterAction. *Diversity in Development: U.S. Voluntary Assistance to Africa.* New York: InterAction, 1985.

——. *Southern Africa Development News*. (Annual subscription $50 for six issues)

Jacobs, Dan. *The Brutality of Nations*. New York: Knopf, 1987.

Sinclair, Michael. *Community Development in South Africa: A Guide for American Donors*. Washington, DC: Investor Responsibility Research Center, Inc., 1986.

Sindab, Jean, ed. *The Churches' Search for Justice and Peace in Southern Africa*. Geneva, Switzerland: World Council of Churches, 1987.

United Nations Children's Fund. *Children on the Front Line: The Impact of Apartheid, Destabilization, and Warfare on Children in Southern and South Africa*. New York and Geneva: UNICEF, 1987.

Timberlake, Lloyd. *Africa in Crisis: The Causes, the Cures of Environmental Bankruptcy*. London: Earthscan, 1985.

U.S. Committee for Refugees. "Beyond the Headlines: Refugees in the Horn of Africa." Washington, DC: U.S. Committee for Refugees, 1988.

——. "Refugees from Mozambique: Shattered Land, Fragile Asylum." Washington, DC: U.S. Committee for Refugees, 1986.

VI. Central America

The Inter-Hemispheric Education Resource Center does research and publications on Central American aid issues, such as *The New Right Humanitarians* and *Low-Intensity Conflict: The New Battlefield in Central America* (1986). Currently in preparation are materials on PVOs, churches, and the Religious Right in Central America. (Box 4506, Albuquerque, NM 87196)

Oxfam America. "Contradictions and Inconsistencies in Humanitarian Assistance to the Contras." Boston: Oxfam America, 1986.

Pilon, Juliana Geron. "Are United Nations Camps Cheating Refugees in Honduras?" Washington, DC: The Heritage Foundation, 1984.

U. S. Agency for International Development. *Displaced Persons in El Salvador: An Assessment*. Washington, DC: 1984.

U.S. Committee for Refugees. "Aiding the Desplazados of El Salvador: The Complexity of Humanitarian Assistance." Washington, DC: U.S. Committee for Refugees, 1984.

Walker, Thomas W., ed. *Reagan versus the Sandinistas: The Undeclared War on*

Nicaragua. Boulder, Colorado: Westview Press, 1987.

VII. Asia and the Middle East

Bello, Walden. *U.S. Sponsored Low-Intensity Conflict in the Philippines.* San Francisco: Institute for Food and Development Policy, forthcoming.

Charney, Joel R., and Spragens, John Jr. *Obstacles to Recovery in Vietnam and Kampuchea: U.S. Embargo of Humanitarian Aid.* Boston: Oxfam America, 1984.

Fernando, Mervyn. "Global Violence and Racial Violence in Sri Lanka." *Logos Magazine,* December 1986 (Center for Society and Religion, 281 Deans Road, Colombo 10, Sri Lanka).

Jackson, Tony. "Just Waiting to Die? Cambodian Refugees in Thailand." Oxford, England: Oxfam U.K., 1987.

Levy, Barry S., and Susott, Daniel C., eds., *Years of Horror, Days of Hope: Responding to the Cambodian Refugee Crisis.* Millwood, N.Y., New York City, and London: Associated Faculty Press, 1987.

Mason, Linda A., and Brown, Roger. *Rice, Rivalry, and Politics.* Notre Dame, Indiana: University of Notre Dame Press, 1983.

Phillips, James A. "Updating U.S. Strategy for Helping Afghan Freedom Fighters." Washington, DC: The Heritage Foundation, 1986.

Scoble, Harry M., and Wiseberg, Laurie S., eds. *Access to Justice: The Struggle for Human Rights in South East Asia.* London: Zed Books, Ltd., 1985.

Shawcross, William. *The Quality of Mercy.* New York: Simon and Schuster, 1984.

APPENDIX VI
INTERACTION MEMBER AGENCIES

Adventist Development and Relief International
African Medical and Research Foundation
Africare
Aga Khan Foundation USA
Air Serv International
America's Development Foundation
American Council for Nationalities Service
American Friends Service Committee
American Fund for Czechoslovak Refugees
American Jewish Joint Distribution Committee
American Jewish World Service
American Near East Refugee Aid
American ORT Federation
American Red Cross
American Refugee Committee
Americares Foundation
Baptist World Alliance
Breakthrough Foundation
Brother's Brother Foundation
Buddhist Council for Refugee Rescue and Resettlement
CARE
Paul Carlson Medical Program
Children International
Children's Survival Fund
Christian Children's Fund
Church World Service, Inc.
CODEL, Inc.
Concern America
Direct Relief International
The End Hunger Network
Eritrean Relief Committee
Esperanca, Inc.
Experiment in International Living
Food for the Hungry, Inc.
Foster Parents Plan
Foundation for International Community Assistance
Foundation for the Peoples of the South Pacific
Freedom From Hunger Foundation
Global Water
Goodwill Industries of America
Grassroots International
Hadassah

Heifer Project International
Helen Keller International
Hermandad
HIAS
The Hunger Project
Institute for International Development
Institute of Cultural Affairs
Interchurch Medical Assistance, Inc.
International Agency for Apiculture Development
International Catholic Migration Commission
International Center for Research on Women
International Eye Foundation
International Institute for Environment and Development
International Institute of Rural Reconstruction
International Rescue Committee
International Social Service/American Branch
International Voluntary Services
Laubach Literacy International
League for International Food Education
Lutheran Immigration and Refugee Service
Lutheran World Relief
MAP International
Mennonite Central Committee
Mennonite Economic Development Associates
Mercy Corps International
Migration and Refugee Services/US Catholic Conference
National Council of Negro Women
Near East Foundation
OEF International
Operation California
Operation Crossroads Africa, Inc.
Opportunities Industrialization Centers International
Overseas Development Council
Oxfam America, Inc.
PACT
Pan American Development Foundation
Partners of the Americas
The Pathfinder Fund
Pax World Foundation
Phelps-Stokes Fund
Planned Parenthood of New York City
Planning Assistance
Polish American Immigration and Relief Committee
Population Communication
Presiding Bishop's Fund for World Relief/Episcopal Church
Project Concern International
Refugees International

Rodale International
St. Mary's Food Bank
Salvation Army World Service Office
Save the Children Federation
SEEDS
Sister Cities International/Technical Assistance Programs
Surgical Aid to Children of the World
Technoserve
Tolstoy Foundation
Trickle Up Program
U.S. Committee for UNICEF
Unitarian Universalist Service Committee
United Israel Appeal
Volunteers in Technical Assistance
Winrock International
World Concern
World Education
World Hunger Year, Inc.
World Neighbors
World Relief Corporation
World Vision
Young Men's Christian Association of the USA
Young Women's Christian Association of the USA